AFRICAN PARENTS MUST KNOW

MUST KNOW

Child Protection and Welfare Issues in the United Kingdom

AFRICAN PARENTS MUST KNOW

Child Protection and Welfare Issues in the United Kingdom

KEMI WILLIAMS

authorHOUSE®

AuthorHouse™
1663 Liberty Drive
Bloomington, IN 47403
www.authorhouse.com
Phone: 1-800-839-8640

This publication is designed to provide authoritative information in regard to the subject matters covered. It is sold with the understanding that the publisher and the author are not engaged in rendering legal or other professional service. If legal advice or other expert assistance is required, the services of a competent professional should be sought.

Published by AuthorHouse   04/03/2013

ISBN: 978-1-4772-4221-6 (sc)
ISBN: 978-1-4772-4222-3 (e)

Any people depicted in stock imagery provided by Thinkstock are models, and such images are being used for illustrative purposes only.
Certain stock imagery © Thinkstock.

This book is printed on acid-free paper.

Because of the dynamic nature of the Internet, any web addresses or links contained in this book may have changed since publication and may no longer be valid. The views expressed in this work are solely those of the author and do not necessarily reflect the views of the publisher, and the publisher hereby disclaims any responsibility for them.

To the King Eternal, Immortal, Invincible, Invisible;
Him who alone is truly wise . . .

TABLE OF CONTENTS

CASE STUDIES

FOREWORD

Understanding the background and diversity of African families and valuing the things that are particularly significant in their lives need careful consideration if meaningful dialogues about their parenting are to be developed. It is important to consider how to sensitively engage in discussions about their beliefs and behaviours concerning child-rearing practices.

Ideas such as affirming some parenting practices, adopting a strengths-based orientation, whilst at the same time ensuring that the welfare of children in need and those at risk of harm are safeguarded and promoted should be encouraged in professional settings.

Needless to say, these are key challenges for social workers and other professionals working cross-culturally. Put very simply, supporting African caregivers to parent effectively requires starting from a place that understands their unique life experiences and values and how these influence their parenting styles. In a context where African parents' care-giving is perceived as deficient, and where they are judged harshly by default, a book written for and about this group of parents is invaluable.

A key issue that often arises in working with some African parents, especially those who have newly arrived in the United Kingdom, is the little knowledge and awareness of the child protection regulations they have. Many fall foul of the law whilst still struggling to understand some of the expectations placed on them by their new environment.

The author, an experienced social worker from an African background, has used her insider knowledge and positioning to highlight the unique challenges of being an African parent in the United Kingdom context, and suggests specific strategies to support parenting. Thus, a central theme of this book is to get African parents to reflect on the ways in which certain environmental factors as well as their own parental behaviours and practices may be harmful to their children's well-being. The book also highlights what is good and valuable about African child-rearing practices, whilst providing useful insights to help parents reflect on parent-child relationships, family relationships, and different cultural practices of child-rearing.

In the sometimes hostile environment of racism, African parents need to nurture their children to develop a positive sense of identity for coping in a society that could devalue them. Tools to help them explore the conditions and experiences that may undermine their ability to maximise their parenting potential, and more importantly, to question practices that may be harmful to their children's development, is to be celebrated. This book is such a tool and is thus warmly welcomed.

I believe this book will help African parents, guardians and caregivers to affirm what they are doing that is of immense benefit to their children, as well as being a useful resource for how to take steps to change practices that may have a negative influence on their children's wellbeing. It will also be a very useful resource for social workers and other professionals that want to understand and support this group of parents and their children better.

Dr Claudia Bernard

Head of Social Work & Postgraduate Research

Goldsmiths, University of London

INTRODUCTION

In the field of child welfare, parents and carers are well-recognised as the single most significant factor in a child's life. They can however still be the most uninformed when it comes to issues regarding children as they apply in a given state. While professionals and others who work with children receive training and information on a regular basis, there is a general lack of awareness amongst many parents in the United Kingdom with regard to child welfare matters.

Traditional parenting skills learnt from their own parents also appear to be no longer sufficient and it is almost compulsory for today's parents to have a greater level of knowledge and skills to parent effectively - especially when living in a different country. This is particularly true for many African parents in the United Kingdom. Some African families have suffered and continue to suffer as a result of this, and African children are becoming increasingly over-represented in local authorities' looked after, child protection and criminal justice systems. It was with these in mind that I wrote this book.

Although this book has been written for African parents, I am aware of and acknowledge the fact that Africans are not a homogenous group. Africa itself is an enormous continent, the second largest in the world, with 54 unique countries, one billion inhabitants and over 3,000 distinct ethnic groups. Africans however constitute what is considered a significant ethnic minority group in the United Kingdom with possibly over one million people excluding those not officially accounted for. The contents of this book will therefore not be relevant to all African parents in the United Kingdom in exactly the same way. It is however still true that many Africans have similar experiences in the United Kingdom due to their heritage, culture, immigrant and minority status.

By and large, this book is meant for African parents in the United Kingdom, but the law, examples, procedures and cases referred to are specific to England and Wales. Scotland and Northern Ireland have different variations of legislation on children which regularly come into play when dealing with child welfare issues.

It is important to say right from the beginning that the majority of African children in the United Kingdom have their needs well met within their families. The greater number of African adults and children in the United Kingdom continue to rise against all odds, doing this great country proud, and have made substantial achievements and tremendous strides in all fields including sports, the media, academia, law and medicine.

There however remains a significant minority of children whose care has been, and is being continuously compromised due to several cultural, societal and environmental factors, as well as a lack of understanding of the prevailing culture and laws in the United Kingdom by their parents.

Knowledge is power and the major catalyst for change. The primary objective is to therefore provide essential information and awareness to African and other immigrant parents on children's issues, to enhance their ability in parenting and to promote their children's wellbeing in a different society. Everyone can however learn something new about children and their welfare in this context. I would therefore encourage you to read this book with the view of gaining fresh insight into an area you may or may not be familiar with.

It is obvious that one book cannot cover absolutely everything that African parents should know. This however serves as a one stop reference manual addressing this very important area. It is written in fourteen easy to read, distinct chapters with case studies. Please note that I have used the male gender ('him' and 'he') in describing the child in general where it is necessary but mean both the male and female child. I hope the information in this book will act as a good knowledge base and become an impetus for change and growth in many African families as well as being a support to the professionals and organisations that work with them.

I particularly desire this to be an empowering tool for African parents in their role of caring for children in a foreign land. I sincerely wish you all the best as you live and parent in the United Kingdom.

Kemi Williams
London, 2013

CHAPTER 1

ARRIVAL IN THE UNITED KINGDOM

There are many issues that immigrants have to contend with on arrival in a foreign country. Some of them come as a complete surprise and culture shock to many whose perspective before arrival was via rose-tinted spectacles.

Many African people who had never visited the United Kingdom before immigrating strongly believed it was in many ways the biblical land of milk and honey. No degree of discouragement from friends or family could dissuade them from embarking on their journey. In any case, many were in such dire straits 'back home' that the grass was in their view, definitely much greener elsewhere.

No consideration or weight is given to the many things that are taken for granted when living in familiar surroundings. Things such as being within a culture that you know, and an informal system that you clearly understand, having your family and friends close by, understanding the language, accent, colloquial expressions and even humour of the people around you, as well as people not asking you to repeat yourself when you speak. In short, not standing out like a sore thumb.

The comfortable familiarity with food, places, names and people, is usually taken for granted when embarking on immigration. Some African immigrants come into the United Kingdom better prepared than others. They have done their homework and research well. They waited patiently, made formal arrangements for work and accommodation, had job interviews and obtained job offers and work permits before commencing their journey. Some were already citizens by virtue of their birth when their own parents studied or lived in the United Kingdom in the 1950s, 60s, 70s and 80s before the automatic citizenship by birth laws changed in 1983, with the British National Act 1981.

> *The comfortable familiarity with food, places, names and people, is usually taken for granted when embarking on immigration.*

Under the Act, children of immigrants were no longer entitled to automatic citizenship by birth from the 1st of January 1983. Some African parents naturalised and became settled immigrants with citizenship status after a period of time, or through marriage. Some fled war-torn countries and other terrible conditions and therefore arrived as asylum seekers and possibly thereafter, were granted refugee status. Whilst many others, with no firm plan in place, yet obsessed with immigrating, resort to almost any means in their quest for a new start in the United Kingdom.

Some Africans have been known to come into the United Kingdom on other people's passports or have obtained visas under false pretences of coming to study or visit. Many others came into the United Kingdom genuinely as students, wanting to improve their qualifications with the intention of returning to their countries after their studies. Some other students study with the hope of regularising their right to remain in the United Kingdom after their studies, find jobs and settle down.

Generally, the vision of many African immigrants is similar; as far as they are concerned, once they got their proverbial foot in the door, or on United Kingdom soil, the rest of their problems would be resolved.

Many African immigrants arrive in the United Kingdom with one or two suitcases, a few contact numbers for people they might or might not know, and a heart full of a mixture of hope and apprehension. Although, the greater number of Africans lived in cities before emigrating, things are different in the United Kingdom. The culture and pace of life are much faster and very different from what they are used to.

One of the things many Africans first struggle with is how everything is perfectly timed and how everyone expects you to arrive on schedule – literally to the minute! There is no such thing as African timing or when the cock crows - in fact, 9am is 8.55am.

Also, in most parts of Africa, women carry themselves gracefully, conscious of their looks and femininity. It is commonly said that African women do not walk - they sway, watching their steps delicately on the way to work or wherever else regardless of their social class, even with a well-balanced basket of wares on their heads. Here in the United Kingdom, especially in the cities, most people have a similar demeanour, men and women alike, walking briskly, in a business-like and often expressionless manner.

Many Africans also soon realise that an invitation to the pub was not an offer for free food or drinks. These are however mundane differences in culture that pale into insignificance as other more substantial issues begin to show up; and these become particularly important when children are involved.

Staying with Family and Friends

Many Africans on arrival in the United Kingdom cannot afford to rent their own accommodation immediately and most start out by staying with family or friends who can only support them for a short period of time. Living with family and friends usually has its difficulties for both hosts and guests. Most guests arrive already anxious about how to settle into the United Kingdom and what the future holds. Being considerate houseguests may not be foremost on their minds. Hosts are also likely to have their own pressures and for most that have lived in the United Kingdom for a while, a high premium is placed on their privacy and a quiet home environment.

Family members and friends who accommodate new arrivals usually accept this as a social and cultural responsibility. The new arrivals on their part may fail to recognise the extent of the sacrifice that the hosts make in accommodating them as the scenario is different from the informal living arrangements that obtain in many parts of Africa. It is therefore important that the new immigrant who is to become a guest is aware of certain factors that could make living with friends and relatives easier in the United Kingdom.

First, if possible, arrangements with hosts should be made before arrival in the United Kingdom. Many guests have been known to arrive unannounced on the doorsteps of unprepared hosts. If the host has a partner, the guest should ensure they are both aware and in agreement to having him in their home. It is also helpful to inform the hosts of the likely length of the stay with them. Hosts need to be kept informed if the situation changes and if the period of stay is likely to be longer than planned.

Second, whilst it would be considered offensive in many parts of Africa for guests to contribute to the household bills and other expenses, it may be covertly welcomed by some hosts in the United Kingdom - especially if they are on a tight financial budget already. Guests should therefore consider offering whatever they can afford as a contribution to the household expenses while they remain there. Even if hosts refuse this sort of offer of support, guests will be considered thoughtful if they look out for household items and groceries that run out and which they can easily replace. It is also important that guests participate in household chores on a regular basis as long as they remain in the home.

Third, guests need to be mindful and respect already established boundaries and routines in the hosts' home. For example, if the hosts do not watch television, play music or entertain guests after a certain time of the day, this should be respected, however stifling it may be to the guests.

These are just a few but important issues guests should be aware of.

Being a Host

An amusing dynamic on United Kingdom roads is the sometimes impatient reaction of many experienced drivers to learner drivers. Many completely forget how petrified they once were themselves wondering if they will ever get it right and pass their driving test. Similarly, it is easy for hosts to forget what it was like for them when they first arrived in the United Kingdom.

Hosts can play a great part in ensuring their guests settle quickly, by sharing their experience and vital information on schools, jobs, housing and other local resources that they are already familiar with. It is important that hosts remember that new immigrants some of who would only begin to look for employment on arrival are unlikely to be able to make significant financial contribution to their upkeep and would need a lot of support at this stage.

Generally, the sooner guests can move out the better it is likely to be for all concerned and their relationship, especially if the hosts are already a family unit. There is a saying that two things stink after three days if not well preserved - fish and a guest/host relationship.

CHAPTER 2

PARENTAL PRESSURES

The role of a parent brings its own pressures whether one is an immigrant or not. Many people, who would not give up their role as parents for any other position in the world, are still surprised at how continuously demanding of all aspects of their resources children can be. Immigrant parents adjusting to a new society, begin to experience an additional set of pressures shortly after arrival regardless of how they came to be in the United Kingdom. Pressures that emerge have an impact on the parent and child as individuals and the family as a whole. Some of these pressures develop almost immediately while others build up over time, become multi-faceted, complex and often manifest as serious problems. Some of the significant pressures faced by immigrating Africans include some of those discussed below.

Housing

Housing is one of the major areas that need to be sorted out if the plan is to remain in the United Kingdom long-term. Housing and the living environment are more important than many give them credit for. They have a great impact on the physical and mental wellbeing of adults and children. It is a well-known fact that a child's environment has a huge bearing on his development and learning. Good housing and a good home-learning environment have been proven to aid educational attainment. Inadequate housing continues to be a major stressor with regard to children and families' welfare in African communities in the United Kingdom.

Most parts of Africa practice a collectivist culture, which means that communal living and sharing the space in a home with other family members was encouraged and an individualist culture as it obtains in the United Kingdom, such as having your own space or room as an individual was discouraged and considered selfish in many situations. It is therefore very rarely considered to be a need for a child to have a room or even a bed to himself in the home in several African communities except in wealthy families. Many children growing up in Africa share a room with several other siblings and relatives and sometimes may even share a bed with a sibling or two. None of these practices - individualist or collectivist - is right or wrong; and they both have their pros and cons.

In the United Kingdom, sharing, as is common in Africa, would be considered overcrowding and inappropriate for children. Parents in the United Kingdom should therefore be careful in limiting themselves and their children to how most families lived in Africa, as children are likely to become uncomfortable and resentful over time, growing up in such circumstances.

For example, here in the United Kingdom, it could be considered inappropriate for a child of a certain age not to have his own bed, or to have to share a room or bed with his parents, opposite sex siblings or extended family members. Such practices are regarded as normal in many parts of Africa.

Social Housing: Social housing is generally provided by local authorities and not-for-profit organisations such as housing associations, sometimes called Registered Social Landlords

(RSL). They are subsidised by the State and let at low rent to people in housing need.

The laws, policies and guidance on housing in the United Kingdom have evolved significantly in recent years. Currently, there are stricter eligibility criteria for the little local authority social housing (council houses) that remain as policies have changed and many have been sold to long-term tenants. Demand however continues to rise even as supply has dwindled. Individuals and families still need to apply through their local authorities and have their needs assessed to get accommodation through an RSL.

The stamp on arrival on many passports from Africa stating 'Nil recourse to public funds' (NRPF) also limits many from attempting to apply for these forms of subsidised housing in the first instance or for welfare benefits to supplement their rent. Even if you were a UK-born immigrant with citizenship status, there is still the habitual resident test to pass before you can have recourse to public funds or benefits which social housing falls under. Generally, the test applies to anyone who arrived in the United Kingdom within the two years before making a housing or benefits application.

In deciding habitual residence, the key factors are length, continuity and general nature of actual residence, but intentions are also considered. For example, a person who is in a form of long-term permanent employment shortly after they arrive in the United Kingdom is very likely to be deemed to have passed the test as their employment suggests an intention to be habitually resident in the United Kingdom. Another person may not be deemed habitually resident if they are not in employment and travel in and out of the United Kingdom often, even if they have been in the United Kingdom for a few years.

Private Renting: Many people rent from private landlords and as with all forms of housing, it has its advantages and disadvantages. The rent is usually much higher than renting from a social landlord and several landlords require initial deposits which many new immigrants cannot afford to pay. Genuine landlords who are willing to offer a proper tenancy agreement are also the ones more likely to demand proper references and guarantees from credible people who the immigrant may not have immediate access to. Advantages of renting privately include having a wider choice in terms of the type of accommodation and area you would like to live in.

The fortunate immigrants, when it comes to addressing their housing needs, are those who are better prepared financially, and these include people that come in with job offers from employers who support their process of accommodation in one way or the other. Landlords are more willing to rent to those with a regular source of income and to those who have convincing evidence that rents would be paid as agreed. Some landlords let out flats or single rooms at exorbitant prices to immigrants who have no recourse to public funds, often in overcrowded conditions and without a proper secure tenancy agreement in place.

As you will probably appreciate, it will be easier for a legal immigrant to resolve their housing issues sooner than those with an unresolved immigration status. Some parents however sacrifice good accommodation for other priorities without considering its significance or impact on their children.

Advice: Do not be discouraged if your housing situation is currently not what you would like it to be. Find out if you are eligible for welfare support, such as housing benefit, as soon as possible. Get the best housing you can afford as soon as you can. Do your research, not just on the house but the area you plan to move to - especially with regards to schools and other amenities. There are areas in the United Kingdom that are generally safer and have better schools than others.

As for social housing, you may be entitled to more than you think. In fact, your rights and entitlements may change with time. So while you may not be entitled to support with your housing at one stage, you may, over a period of time, become eligible due to several factors, including for example, the size of your family, the ages, gender and particular needs of your children and other household members. You could also partition bigger rooms in your home to give older children some privacy - of course with permission from the landlord.

Before entering into a tenancy agreement with a landlord, check the agreement carefully and ask questions about anything you are not sure of. You may want to seek legal advice or consult experienced housing advisers. There are many local community law centres, citizens' advice bureaux (CAB) and housing rights services where you can get advice for free. Information about them and other services are also available in local libraries, the local Yellow Pages or via the internet.

Always remember that the rights laid down by law always override those which are stated in a written or oral agreement. An agreement which suggests that you or your landlord have fewer or more rights or responsibilities than those provided by common law or statute will therefore be a sham tenancy agreement and consequently null and void. The regulations governing access to housing and other public services can be complex so it is important to get advice on your own individual circumstances.

Buying Your Own Home: Owning your own house or flat is probably the ultimate, where housing is concerned. In the United Kingdom, this is usually done by taking out a huge loan called a mortgage either from banks or other financial institutions and then making monthly payments with interest to the lender in order to pay off the loan. Usually a substantial deposit is required and most lenders will only grant a mortgage to individuals who are permanently resident in the United Kingdom or have the right to remain in the United Kingdom indefinitely. Buying your own home is perhaps one of the most exciting but also likely to be the most expensive financial decision you will ever make. It is a long term financial commitment, lasting in most cases up to twenty-five years.

You should seek advice from and endeavour to use the services of reputable financial advisers and brokers. This can become invaluable in getting the best from the often confusing market and process of buying a property. It is always wise to look before you leap and consider all the obligations you will have to meet as a home owner. Many people have 'bought' and 'lost' their homes because they could not afford the repayments when their circumstances changed for the worse.

Apart from mortgage repayments which may fluctuate with interest rates, you will become responsible for all the costs of maintaining the property, including major structural repairs, routine repairs and improvements. You will also need to take other costs into consideration such as; mortgage protection insurance in case you should fall ill or lose your job, life insurance to enable your family pay off the mortgage if you die before repayment of the loan, building insurance against structural repairs, contents insurance against the risk of theft, fire, flood or other accidents, as well as the normal costs of council tax, water rates, gas, electricity, telephone, etc.

Ground rent, leasehold and service charges may also apply, especially if you are buying a flat. As part of the process of buying a house or flat you may also need to pay for: a solicitor or licensed conveyancer, an independent survey, the mortgage to be arranged, the land registry fee and stamp duty.

As a tenant, you may be able to claim housing benefit to help with the rent. As an owner-occupier, you will not receive any housing benefit to help with your mortgage costs. You may be entitled to income support to assist with housing costs, but this is not usually payable for several months after you first claim it. Do not forget to also take time out to meet the neighbours and learn a bit more about them and the neighbourhood, before making a final decision in buying the property.

Employment and Income

We live in dire times and unemployment affects both indigenous citizens and immigrants alike. However for the African immigrant who for several reasons is more likely to be unemployed in a competitive field, the situation could be more heightened. There is also a higher likelihood of these immigrants taking lower paid jobs than they are qualified for, thereby becoming under-employed.

One of the major concerns for most immigrant Africans is the lack of recognition for the qualifications they have obtained in Africa or the need to convert most of these qualifications to acceptable ones by taking conversion examinations and tests. This invariably leads to a level of poverty for many, at least for a period of time when they are not gainfully employed. These Africans are more likely to work unsociable hours and long shifts for a paycheque that many indigenes would find unacceptable. This could also lead to having to take on more than one job to make ends meet, which often causes stress for parents and could affect the care of the children.

Many Africans also have immediate and extended families they still provide for 'back home' – families who may not understand their predicament in the United Kingdom. African immigrants are also likely to be juggling study, work and family life all at the same time. In any case, many have to work, not only to sustain themselves and their family, but also to pay for their studies, which for some gave them the right to be in the United Kingdom in the first place.

Many others have restricted employment status; some have to work to remain in the United Kingdom. For some, their employment is tied to their immigration status and their immigration status may be tied to their employment - a typical catch-22 situation. You do not need to look too closely to see how this could have an impact on African parents and their children.

Advice: You are less likely to be discriminated against and are more likely to find employment when your skills are in demand. If you have a choice, train and work in a field where there is a high demand for particular skills. Currently in the United Kingdom, you are more likely to find a job within communities in one of the caring professions, than as a solicitor in the city even if you are highly qualified and experienced.

You may also consider starting a business at home and this may be easier than you think. Most local authorities have support in place for those starting small businesses and can provide information and support in many areas including setting up, self-employment and tax liability issues.

For example, some stay-at-home parents with the right skills, space and appropriate facilities in their home can register to be child-minders or foster carers, by going through some training and checks required by their local authorities. The African community itself is very large and there are many areas of need which you can meet as a business. If you have the right skills you may be able to make or mend clothes, fix people's hair, collect people's children from school, prepare African dishes for busy families on a weekly/monthly basis; clean, repair and decorate their homes or be a tutor to their children.

Africans are very creative and many have become successful in various areas of business in the United Kingdom. There are many things you can do to earn a living or an extra income, but you have to think about it, put clear plans and strategies in place, and be ready to work hard at it. You need to ask yourself, "what needs are out there that I can meet?" Remember, that even in a recession, people still spend money, they are just more careful about it. You may also start a web-based business. Think outside the box and even the sky may not be your limit.

Isolation and Poor Social Support

Shortly after settling in the United Kingdom, it gradually begins to dawn on parents that on many occasions they are lonely and alone. Many African immigrants do not anticipate or they under-estimate the extent of the cultural differences with regard to the lack of social support that they might face in a new country.

Several married couples arrive separately over a period of time, or in some cases the other spouse does not have the opportunity or privilege to immigrate at all. This then leads to an enforced single status in the United Kingdom for many. In many cases, there are no friends, family or neighbours to drop the children off with or to help pick them up from school when parents go to work, shopping and other outings.

Most of the readily available support is formal and has to be paid for. With a tight budget and with several immigrants not entitled to state benefits, formal childcare support such as private nurseries and registered child-minders may not be a viable option for many. People then begin to realise how different things have become from the slow-paced life in many parts of Africa, where some neighbours were as close as members of their family, to a place where nobody has time for chit-chat and where everyone seems to be in a hurry. The effect of the isolation can have further implications and far-reaching consequences.

Many African immigrants may be in a more favourable situation where, apart from working, they settle quickly into a church, mosque, club or other small community group where the people are friendly enough to want to get to know them. Even then the support received from these groups is usually insufficient in meeting most of their needs. Everybody is busy and working hard to make a living.

What happens then, when your spouse is still 'back home' or has a job that keeps him out of the house for very long hours, or you are a single parent, and the only job you can get is shift work which sometimes starts as early as 7am and the children's school does not start until 9am?

Anybody can find themselves in this predicament whether an immigrant or an indigene. An indigene is however likely to have available to them a network of support they have built over time. They are more likely to have generations of family members, friends and acquaintances who are not caught up in the immigrant rat race and who can offer a helping hand every now and again. They may also have the privilege of considering some jobs unsuitable and remain on government welfare allowances and benefits to meet their needs, while caring for their children, whilst an immigrant may have no access to such benefits and has to stay employed as a condition for his or her right to remain in the United Kingdom.

CASE 1- POOR SOCIAL SUPPORT

Nyasha is a 38 year old immigrant from Zimbabwe who came into the United Kingdom on a recruitment programme for nurses six months ago. She lost her husband three years ago in a car crash and was pleased with the prospects of a new start in a new country. She decided to bring her only child, Rudo, who just turned five, with her to the United Kingdom in spite of her mother's offer to continue caring for Rudo in Zimbabwe while she, Nyasha, settled.

She was able to register Rudo at a local school in the south-east of London not far from her rented accommodation and the local hospital where she is now employed. Nyasha became very concerned when she was completing the school forms and needed to add the names of two local people the school could contact in an emergency apart from her.

The only people Nyasha knew well enough were two friends and a family member from Zimbabwe. Unfortunately, although they lived in the United Kingdom, they were all settled outside of the London area and could not be classified as 'living locally' or contactable in an emergency. Nyasha only started work three weeks ago and had attended the local church once. Although the people at work and the local church were friendly, she did not think it was appropriate to ask for what she considered to be a personal and private issue. The neighbourhood she lived in was quiet and she had, only on a couple of occasions, caught fleeting glances of her neighbours in the block of flats where she lived.

What would you do about getting emergency contact numbers for your child's school if you were in Nyasha's shoes?

CASE 2 - POOR SOCIAL SUPPORT

Bolanle arrived in the United Kingdom with her two young sons, 2 year old Joel and 4 year old Sammy, four months ago from Nigeria. She was already a citizen of the United Kingdom, having been born by parents who studied here in the 1960s. She was excited about the prospects of getting a job as a project manager soon and the likely arrival of her husband, Kayode, in a few months, if she got the job.

She had prepared well for this particular job interview and was now smartly dressed in her new suit, ready to drop off her two young sons at a child-minder's who she had arranged to care for them for the day. She whistled as she walked along with her two sons. She was almost sure she would get the job as the manager had shown a lot of interest in her curriculum vitae (CV) and past experiences and they seemed to have got on well at the first interview. The manager had also called her twice, asking if she was prepared to start work the following week.

On arrival at the front door of the child-minder, she saw a note with her name on it. In the note, the child-minder explained that she had tried calling Bolanle twice but it went to her voicemail. She had to attend to an emergency situation and she did not know when she would be back. Bolanle stood still, thought long and hard for about two minutes, and then headed for the train station with the children. She was desperate for the job and did not want to put off her prospective employers by cancelling or postponing. She took the children with her for the interview in a palatial office complex in a busy part of the city. She explained her predicament to the receptionist who she considered to be the kindest person on earth when she agreed to keep an eye on Sammy and Joel while she went in for her 45-minute interview slot.

Did she do the right thing?

Advice: No man is an island and you will always need people around you especially when you have young children. It is therefore wise and important to begin to build your own support network. It is advisable to be proactive and friendly. Make friends with your children's school-mates' parents, neighbours, members of your faith and community groups and other people with whom you can be mutually supportive and share childcare and baby-sitting arrangements.

You may also want to get to know a few registered child-minders in your area. Many are understanding and flexible with parents' working patterns. You can get a list of registered child-minders and nurseries in your area from your local library, local authority's main office or website. Many parents use a mixture of resources to meet their young children's weekly care needs when they are working and these include family, friends, nurseries and child-minders. It is important that you make sure arrangements are safe and adequate, especially when leaving your children in informal arrangements such as with family and friends.

Discrimination

There are many positive things about living in the United Kingdom; discrimination is not one of them. For most Africans, their experience of discrimination manifests in racism. Many other people will perhaps experience discrimination due to their age, gender, sexuality, socio-economic class or disability. We however still live in a society where a person's skin colour makes a difference to how they are perceived and treated. Racism is therefore a very significant factor that puts African parents under pressure in the United Kingdom, and most are totally unprepared for it.

Racism is a phenomenon that affects everyone, whether in terms of creating and maintaining unearned privileges for some; creating social, economic, and health disparities for many; and segregating or dividing a society into the 'haves' and 'have-nots' with regard to income, education, health, government representation and political voice. Racism is complex and it involves both conscious and unconscious forms of discrimination and institutionalisation. Racism is usually defined on three levels: personal, cultural and institutional.

Personal Racism: The personal is purely related to actions from or by individuals. For example, a neighbour or passer-by may make a racist comment or take negative action towards you and your children just because of your skin colour.

Cultural Racism: The cultural usually manifests itself on a higher level. It usually shows up in the set-up of the society as a whole. It is what is sometimes considered as the standards for appropriate behaviour reflecting the norms and values of the dominant white race. Accepted ways of behaviour in cultures vary, and it is the major factor in perpetuating the cultural level of racism. You are expected to behave in a certain way (social norms) and the society is set up or has evolved to function with those social norms. People who behave differently from the norm may therefore be treated less favourably. For example, many African cultures place a huge emphasis on respecting and deferring to elders with appropriate non-verbal signs of respect shown to them by children or younger people. Children in some African families could therefore be expected to be quiet before elders and not maintain eye contact when speaking. This sort of practice could be deemed oppressive, bad or wrong in the United Kingdom where there is a strong culture of equality between children and adults.

Institutional Racism: The institutional or structural level of racism became popularly understood after the inquest into the death of Stephen Lawrence in 1999. The Macpherson Report following the inquiry defined institutional racism as:

> The collective failure of an organisation to provide an appropriate and professional service to people because of their colour, culture or ethnic origin. It can be seen or detected in processes, attitudes and behaviour which amount to discrimination through unwitting prejudice, ignorance, thoughtlessness and racist stereotyping which disadvantage minority ethnic people.

The Macpherson Report concluded at the time that institutional racism was entrenched in the Police Force, and this prevented the Stephen Lawrence case from being fairly investigated. It was also recognised that the Police Force was not the only institution in which racism was present.

Virtually all recognised organisations and institutions are now required to and have adopted strong equality and anti-discriminatory policies to prevent racism in their employment and promotion of staff and in the provision of services. A lot of progress has been made in many institutions, but the United Kingdom is still a long way from ensuring that discriminatory practices and racism are stamped out in practice and from people's day-to-day experience.

Many Africans will experience racism in one form or the other after a few years of being in the United Kingdom. In recent times in the United Kingdom, there has been an increasing level of zero tolerance by authorities towards racist acts, slurs and remarks

...increasing levels of sophistication and civilisation, appears to have made racism more subtle and covert.

that are blatant - these are likely to be considered racist crimes. This, as well as increasing levels of sophistication and civilisation, appears to have made racism more subtle and covert.

Subtle Racism: Subtle forms of racism can sometimes seem impossible or is the most difficult type to address or prove. In many instances, the cost of fighting the injustice is so high in time, emotion and monetary terms that many let it pass unchallenged. Subtle racism can manifest in, for example, not regarding black people as equals, ignoring them, ridiculing them or making snide remarks, gestures and comments. For example, a teacher who is racist and does not like black children, will teach them alongside their white counterparts, but may ignore their attempts to answer questions, laugh at their mistakes, punish them excessively, and not encourage them to do well and achieve.

Because the behaviour is usually covert, it can be difficult to prove. Unfortunately, this all adds to the internal conflicts and feelings of helplessness and anger many immigrants feel. Knowing you are being treated less favourably, simply because of your colour whilst struggling with other areas of life, can be a difficult thing to experience and to cope with.

There is another form of racism which appears to have become worse than those defined above and that is;

Internalised Racism: This manifests when members of a stigmatised race, accept negative messages about their own abilities and intrinsic worth. It is more covert in many adults, but the multi-layered effects of internalised racism on African children are showing up in more overt ways.

Many African adults for example may begin to see or think of themselves as stupid, lazy, unimportant, inarticulate or inferior to their white counterparts. African parents may not see their own views and opinions as valuable and find they are unable to express their point of view or even apologise for having one. The unresolved immigration status of many can make this worse as they attempt to be as invisible as possible in the system, trying hard not to draw attention to themselves and keeping within the confines of the law.

Children of African heritage on the other hand, may begin to turn on each other, mistreating themselves and other members of their group in similar ways to their own mistreatment as the targets of racism.

It is important for Africans to understand how racism can affect them and their children - especially on the internal level. Unfortunately, following many bad experiences, children see the system as *them versus us*. The children, especially teenage black boys, believe nobody respects them or cares, and so they begin to show that they do not care for or respect people either. They think no one believes they can achieve, and so they make no effort at achieving. They want respect and think it can be gained by instilling fear in others. The younger generation is usually the direct opposite to their parents when it comes to dealing with racism of any kind. They may even begin to see their parents' covert expression of internalised racism as weak and lily-livered and they may not fully understand why their parents cannot stand up for themselves.

They demand to be heard and some will begin to fight what they see as injustice in a blatant, rebellious and even criminal manner. Unfortunately, all they end up achieving is attract to themselves negative attention through the media and the criminal justice system. More and more, we see this *'them versus us'* syndrome develop into smaller groups of gang culture.

Unable to fight a system, they turn on each other in order to exert control. Internalised racism, though not the only reason, is part of the reason why many black children are physically attacking and killing each other, playing out their rage about racism at one another. African parents need to remind themselves and their children that in their stance against racism, oppression or discrimination of any kind, their voices and their pens will always be mightier than the sword. The biggest 'racist wars' were fought and won and continue to be best fought, not with guns and knives, but with words and the power of the media.

Advice: Try to explain the concept of racism to your children as they grow up without showing or displaying hostility to the white majority. Explain how ignorance is one of the major causes of racism and help your children to address forms of discrimination when they can. Remind them that they live in an imperfect world with people in various groups often discriminated against and marginalised for example, women, the elderly and the disabled. Help your children to see how other Africans and black people have risen above racism in many ways and continue to do so. Help them to know that they too can rise above it by defying the status quo albeit in appropriate ways. If you can, get involved in the Black History Month in your child's school or within your local community or faith group. Teach your children to write about issues that bother them in a poem, a song, a book, a blog, on social media and in other positive ways.

Incidents of racism, subtle or otherwise may have a powerful impact on a person's mental health and general wellbeing. It is therefore important that it is not continually swept under the carpet. As an adult, do not feel you have to respond to every incident you encounter, but equally, do not suppress your instinct either. If and when you can, confront racist behaviour in a calm manner without accusing the person of being racist. Do so when the opportunity arises and when it is safe to do so. Addressing the particular behaviour could at least help perpetrators to think about why they have treated you differently, or what they have done or said, and hopefully prevent it from being repeated next time.

Racist acts against individuals and groups are crimes under United Kingdom laws and should be reported to the police. There is usually a higher penalty for criminal acts that have connotations of racism than those that do not. It is important to seek formal support or legal advice if you feel you are suffering from the effect of discrimination in a work environment. Start by making an effort to understand your employment guidelines as they relate to your employer's equality and diversity policy. Every organisation should have one and this ought to help you to know what to do and the right steps to take when you feel you are discriminated against or harassed.

It is also important to know that on the personal level, millions of people in the white majority are not racists and that the racists represent a nasty minority. Also remind yourself and your children that some of what is considered as personal racism can be abated through personal conduct and behaviour. Behaviour such as talking over another person or speaking loudly on top of one's voice may be perceived negatively by others, and affect the way people respond to or treat you and your children. Most people are wary of people they perceive as different until they get to know them. As an immigrant you are expected to adapt to a certain extent by understanding the culture of the new country you have adopted.

Marital Conflicts

There are many well-documented advantages to being married. This includes being an ameliorating factor for isolation and loneliness and an opportunity for love, sex and companionship. Many couples however find their roles changing when they arrive in the United Kingdom. A couple which does not adjust quickly to the reality of life in a different culture and economy are likely to end up with serious marital conflicts, sometimes leading to domestic violence as well as separation and or divorce.

In most parts of Africa, a man is the head of his home and the king of his castle in many ways. The traditional African system is to his advantage and he is treated with the respect of a leader, especially within his home. It is not common, whether in a rich, average or poor African household, for a married man to come back home after a day's work to cook his own meal and begin household chores or attend to childcare duties. He will usually be able to kick off his shoes and relax while he waits for his meal. Household chores are seen as women and children's business even without the presence of domestic help. Everyone knows their roles, and there is little overlap.

A man who cannot provide financially for his household is simply not regarded as, a proper man, and a woman who cannot keep the house clean and tidy and ensure her children and husband are provided regular nutritious meals is equally simply regarded as, not a proper woman. In most African countries, even in situations where the woman is in paid employment, she will usually have younger relatives or domestic servants who help out and significantly reduce the pressure on her. It is unlikely that there was friction over roles which were quite clear and simple to understand - until the couple arrive in the United Kingdom.

The culture shock in this area for many African parents especially the men, can be enormous as the known and familiar context of their manhood and fatherhood change and become defined by another culture, in this case, that of the United Kingdom. It is possible that it is the man who first arrives in the United Kingdom before his wife and children join him. It is also possible that the wife arrives first, gets a job and settles quickly before the husband arrives; or perhaps they arrive together but she is able to get a job before him. It only stands to reason that he should take on the role of a house-husband to an extent by helping out with household chores and childcare. While some are able to take this situation in their stride and make changes as necessary, many are not able to manage the internal and external factors that stand as an affront to their previously well-defined roles.

This can become more difficult if there is pressure from ill-informed family members and friends within and outside the United Kingdom who give advice based on their traditional African system; for example, expecting the man to exert manly control, without regard to the reality of life in the United Kingdom. The situation can begin to have a huge psychological impact on the ego of most African men, their self-esteem and daily functioning. Every request from the often over-worked wife concerning housework or children could be seen by him as rude or an insult. The woman is also stressed and anxious; she is not used to taking on the role of provider as well as coming back home to be a cleaner, cook, wife and mother.

Even when the couple are both gainfully employed, many women find they are taking on, in many cases, an equal share or more of the financial household burden quite unlike the reality for many when they were back home in Africa. It therefore stands to reason from her perspective, that without extra help from elsewhere, all other responsibilities in the home should be shared. The woman then begins to stand up to the man, and her humble requests for help with household chores can become, from the husband's viewpoint, incessant demands and nagging.

Many men may see the problem as a relocation issue. In his view, his wife has changed for the worse because they are in a society that is more supportive of women than men. He questions and attacks the new 'feminist' stance his wife is taking. Where situations of this kind are not resolved with practical wisdom, patience and understanding on both sides, serious marital conflicts which have dire consequences on the children and the whole family can occur.

There are many other variants to pressure on the relationships of African couples. Other common occurrences are when couples have broken up due to enforced estrangement when an immigrant cannot raise the funds to bring his family to join him, where one spouse has been unable to obtain the right to enter the United Kingdom or when one of them has been deported. Sometimes it is the pressure of everyday life and the continuous demands of twenty-first century living that is poised to snuff the life out of marital relationships leading to breakups.

It is worth remembering that fathers who have good relationships with the mother of their children are more likely to be involved with and spend time with the children, thereby raising children who are more psychologically and emotionally stable. A mother who feels appreciated and understood by the father of her children is more likely to be a better mother.

Difficulties and friction between parents also tend to divert attention from the children. Couples have to be proactive and methodical in looking out for each other and making their relationship work. It is worth remembering that one of the best gifts in life that parents can give their children is that of a stable two-parent family. Whilst this may be out of some parents' control, as many factors make this ideal impossible to attain in some families, it is a goal well worth striving for in many situations for the children's sake.

Advice: It is important for couples to recognise and evaluate the impact of their current environment on their relationship and family life. Most couples in the United Kingdom have to depend heavily on each other as the major source of support. One of the advantages of the westernised lifestyle is that many couples have become closer in this regard, sharing all aspects of their lives including various chores such as the school run, shopping, cooking and cleaning.

A lot of couples may however find they are unable to resolve conflicts or agree on issues arising from their current situation. If the situation between them cannot be resolved within a reasonable time-frame, it is better for them to seek external support. Whilst many couples want to maintain their privacy, it is healthier to agree to seek appropriate help than for the situation to escalate out of the control of either party.

Many African parents belong to faith groups that provide support and counselling for couples. There are also many organisations that provide professional couple-counselling in the United Kingdom. Unfortunately many charge a fee which can be quite expensive for many immigrants. Some however accept means-tested charges, which is to say that they charge you according to your income or negotiate a fee (see the resource section at the end of this book). Even in situations where the marital relationship has broken down, it is always best to try to maintain as amicable a relationship as possible in order to prevent further distress to the children especially where it comes to arranging contact with the absent parent and agreeing on how their financial needs will be met.

Immigration Issues

Some emigrations from Africa are not well-planned. Many Africans are therefore living in the United Kingdom with unresolved immigration status. Some have pending applications as asylum seekers at the Home Office, some have become over-stayers or have simply become lost in the system, as their student or tourist visas have expired. Some had even entered the country with false documentations in the first place.

Many, as stated earlier did not consider how the situation they now face would be resolved before leaving Africa, but felt it would be sorted out somehow. Many who have used false documentation or other people's identities are now, not only at risk of deportation but also at risk of arrest, conviction and imprisonment for identity fraud, assisting illegal immigration or obtaining leave to remain by deception.

The sad part of this is that many otherwise, law-abiding Africans do not realise that the aforementioned can be crimes punishable by imprisonment. In their view, the only thing they are at risk of is deportation. Most work at two or three menial jobs, keep a low profile, and hope and pray that they will one day, find a 'good lawyer' who will be able to turn their situation around. They are doing what they can to get by and make a living for themselves and their families. Their view is that they are not hurting anyone. After all, they even pay tax out of their wages. They therefore see the United Kingdom immigration laws which can lead to imprisonment in this regard, as 'wicked and unfair'.

An unresolved immigration status also affects a person's ability to be gainfully employed or housed, especially in the current dire economic climate. It also leads to a fear of authority figures and many Africans with such unresolved immigration status are unwilling to report crimes against them to the police. There is a strong need to tell lies, and since it is far easier to tell the truth and remember it than to tell a lie, it leaves people psychologically, mentally and emotionally drained.

There is a story of a lady called Lucy. This was not her real name, but the name she used at employment agencies, whilst looking for work, because of her immigration status. When it was her turn to be interviewed, several members of staff called out "Lucy"! She did not respond, just sat there looking at them quizzically, wondering where this Lucy was until she suddenly remembered that it was supposed to be her name!

The stress heightens, when children have to be coached on what to say about their status and other such personal family details. It becomes worse when the child has to explain why he cannot participate in a school trip to Europe for example, because of his unresolved status. It can have a huge impact on a child's self-esteem and functioning when he is left out of important events without any clear explanation to give his peers and teachers. Several Africans have been duped of thousands of pounds they have worked hard for by unscrupulous employers and immigration solicitors taking advantage of their circumstances and knowing full well their clients will not be able to report the crime to the appropriate authorities or take legal action against them.

For many African parents struggling to bring up children with their unresolved immigration status, going back home to Africa, in their view is not an option. Many have far too many dependants in Africa looking to them for support. Many would find it extremely shameful to return without the Golden Fleece they left in search of, to face the family and friends they left behind.

The situation is made worse by many Africans not being willing or unable to share the reality they are facing in the United Kingdom with their relatives back in Africa, who in many cases are unlikely to believe them anyway. Many others are genuinely fleeing persecution in their country and consider it unsafe to return despite their failed asylum application. Several parents therefore resort to desperate means to survive, and may have to change jobs or move accommodation frequently, thereby disrupting schooling, recreation and provision of essential care for vulnerable young children.

On the 20th of June 2011, it was reported in the news that an illegal immigrant slashed his throat in the airport as he was being deported from London. He survived the self-harm but clearly considered his being dead in the United Kingdom better than being alive in his country.

Concerns have also been raised about removal agents using excessive force in the deportation of illegal immigrants. In July 2011, Amnesty International reported how private security companies use dangerous and improper control and restraint techniques on flights which could lead to loss of life as in the case of 46 year old Jimmy Mubenga, a husband and father of five children in 2010. Jimmy Mubenga was being forcibly removed to Angola, his home country. He passed out and died on the plane whilst being forcibly restrained by three agents.

I also recall being on a flight with a woman being deported with her two children on a flight to Nigeria a few years ago. She was wailing inconsolably as she was being escorted by two removal agents. I had never seen anything like that before and it was a horrific sight; her two young children clung to her looking bewildered. It became unbearable after a while as her crying was distressing to the other passengers on board. It took two 'good Samaritan' women over twenty minutes to console her. These women offered to support her 'back home' and allayed her fears about what was ahead of her. They also raised a huge sum of money on her behalf - collected from willing passengers on the flight. It was one of the most spontaneous and generous acts of charity I had seen in a while, but the effect of that experience on her two children will never be known.

I did not follow up the story, but her outlook and perspective about what lay ahead of her changed somewhat after the intervention of her fellow passengers that day. I observed her as I walked down the aisle shortly afterwards, tucking into her plate of Jollof rice. There is an African saying, which, when translated literarily, says, 'if you can't move forward, at least there must be a way round the back.' Basically, it means, when there is life there is always hope.

Advice: There are many who have been able to resolve their immigration issues legally and obtain the right to remain in the United Kingdom and many who have not. People's circumstances and situations differ and it is always best to seek appropriate legal advice for your own particular situation. Every local authority has community law centres and citizens' advice bureaux where you can receive basic legal advice and link up with other organisations specifically for immigrants.

Being refused asylum and a right to remain is forcing thousands of Africans into abject poverty in the United Kingdom. With no right to work, no recourse to public funds or housing, many Africans are becoming increasingly destitute. The resource section in this book includes the International Organisation for Migration (IOM).

> *Being refused asylum and a right to remain is forcing thousands of Africans into abject poverty in the United Kingdom.*

The organisation supports and helps resettle people who are prepared to voluntarily return to their home countries. They are likely to have their own eligibility criteria of those who qualify for help. There are however many success stories on their website of immigrants who have voluntarily returned and are now gainfully employed, run their own businesses, have become employers themselves and are happy to be back amongst all that is familiar to them. It will most certainly not be an easy process but is probably the best option for many.

Mental Health

Africans are currently over-represented as clients of mental health services in the United Kingdom. One cannot say for sure why this is so, but information from health professionals suggests a strong link between the cultural bereavement and homesickness which many immigrant Africans feel, coupled with some of the other factors we have discussed above which are all major contributory factors in the high rate of mental illness amongst deracinated Africans.

The psychological and disruptive effects of immigration on many individuals cannot be overestimated. It appears therefore that the majority of mental health issues faced by many Africans are psycho-social, rather than genetic. This means that the cause of their illness stems from external, social and environmental factors. Some who had traumatic experiences and came in as asylum seekers also have an added problem if they are experiencing diagnosed or undiagnosed Post-Traumatic Stress Disorder (PTSD).

Many Africans also derive a lot of

> *Mental illness in itself is still poorly understood and even less accepted within African communities and there continues to be a high level of discrimination and stigma attached to it.*

comfort from their faith and religion which may present to those treating mental illnesses as part of the illness. Psychiatric work with immigrant Africans could pose special challenges to indigenous mental health practitioners in the United Kingdom.

There is the compounded difficulty of diagnosing someone of a different cultural background as well as addressing any linked PTSD. Many adult Africans abroad become disillusioned as they get older, and are unable to find the golden opportunities they had dreamt so much about; this also contributes to their mental vulnerability. Mental illness in itself is still poorly understood and even less accepted within African communities and there continues to be a high level of discrimination and stigma attached to it. As with all forms of illness, it is important that appropriate medical advice is sought sooner rather than later.

The above is not an exhaustive list of possible stressors on immigrant African parents. Closely linked to unemployment and low income is the very common pressure of debt.

Loans and Debts

Different kinds of loans can present as an attractive means of getting what you want now, without consideration for how it will be repaid. There are many loan sharks around who prey on individuals who cannot borrow from recognised financial institutions, lending to them at exorbitant interest rates, enforcing repayments by seizure of personal belongings, threats, blackmail and other unconventional means.

Borrowing is currently at an all-time high in the United Kingdom. Many people are struggling to make repayments and most cannot see any light at the end of the tunnel, as they struggle with no income or a low one (which is sometimes inadequate to cover their regular expenses) as well as mounting debts and interest charges. There have been major tragedies with people committing suicide due to the pressure of the huge debts hanging over them like an invisible iron cloak and with loan sharks hounding them.

The rules to observe around loans and debts remain simple, straightforward and timeless. It includes buying only what you can afford to pay off immediately or within a very short period, living within your means and learning to save for what you want to buy in the future. If however you find yourself in debt, it is important not to bury your head in the sand like the proverbial ostrich. I would encourage you to look at the resource section of this book, your local library or the Internet for organisations that provide information, advice and support on debt issues.

Some of the issues raised here can overlap and sometimes present as multi-layered, complex problems for one family. Thus, a parent can be in an underpaid job enduring the trauma of racism, watching their backs at work, on the bus or at the train station and all the time wary of prowling immigration officers who can arrive on a raid at any time. Other problems may include paying dubious immigration lawyers, caring for family 'back home', dealing with poor housing and debts, avoiding authority figures and having to lie at every turn. At the same time they may be suffering from cultural bereavement and home-sickness whilst raising children who are acting out. All these pressures can play a huge and significant part in the African child's welfare.

CASE 3 - MULTIPLE PRESSURES

Ekua Owusu is a 10 year old girl who lives with her parents Joseph and Barbara Owusu and two brothers, 8 year old George and 5 year old David. Ekua moved to the United Kingdom with her parents from Ghana when she was 3 and George was 1 year old. David was born in the United Kingdom after they arrived. The Owusus live in one bedroom of a three-bedroom privately rented accommodation shared with two other families. This is the third house in which they have rented a room over the past seven years.

Barbara has epileptic fits and bi-polar disorder, a mental health condition that affects her moods. Their ongoing immigration and accommodation problems appear to have contributed to Barbara's mental health issues, but one cannot be too sure. Barbara however finds it lonely, missing her family especially her mother terribly, not being able to work because of their unresolved immigration status and finds it continuously uncomfortable and stifling living in one bedroom. Her mental illness makes her suspicious of strangers so she has no friends and remains lonely and isolated whenever her family is not around.

The summer months are usually quite alright for Barbara. She goes out for long walks and sits in the park, but in the winter, she spends all day indoors watching the television in the one bedroom they all share, when the children and Joseph are at school and work. Barbara has put on an incredible amount of weight because of her medication and staying indoors all day.

Joseph Owusu works as a handyman and on occasions as a window cleaner, although he told his family abroad that he is a train driver. Most of the jobs he does are 'cash in hand'. Apart from doing his best to meet his family's basic needs, he pays a huge chunk out of his earnings to immigration lawyers who are trying to sort out his family's immigration status as asylum seekers. He is unaware of any community support that may be available to him and his family and feels it is better he keeps himself and his family out of sight and not draw attention to them.

Ekua is a resilient child and is quite popular at school. She is however ashamed of her family and their situation. Recently, she has begun to bully her classmates, as well as fantasising and lying about her family. She often says they live in a three-bedroom house with a garden and that she has her own room decorated in lilac, her favourite colour. The reality is however the opposite. She shares a room with her parents and two siblings with another child on the way in a house with other strangers using the same bathroom and kitchen facilities. She gets invited to the houses of several of her friends for afternoon teas and sleepovers but has never been able to ask any of her friends to visit her at home.

Ekua's father, Joseph, has had to visit the school twice this term because of her bullying of other children and he has been told she will be excluded from school next time this happens. Ekua told her mother when she got back from school today, that she hates all of them, meaning her parents and siblings and that if they do not move to a house of their own soon, she will run away from home.

CHAPTER 3

Know the Law

**The law of the United Kingdom is not nice when
you fall foul of it.**

[Anonymous]

I found the above quotation funny as there is no place in the world where the law is nice when you fall foul of it. The majority of African parents in the United Kingdom are however so consumed with dealing with the pressures of life in the United Kingdom, that the last thing on their mind is an understanding of the law and culture regarding child welfare issues in the country where they now live.

Most people do not care about such things when what they are grappling with is where to live and how to put food on the table. In discussing this issue with some African parents, I have been told things such as, 'my parents did not need to know much or read a book to bring me up'. What many forget is that not only did they live in a different cultural setting and time, many of their own parents had incredible support in raising their children. Many were raised, cared for and disciplined by a combination of parents, grandparents, other relatives, domestic servants and neighbours with further contributions from the wider community.

As Africans, you need to recognise that you are in a new country, in a different time from when you were parented, and you are required to abide by the laws of the land in which you now live. It is important that you have a clear understanding of the law and cultural values of the country you are now, and the expectations on you as a parent, even if you do not agree with them entirely. You may think, the law is an ass on occasions, but you must also remember that pleading ignorance of the law cannot be an excuse!

I usually use the analogy of the law on driving to drive home my point. In many African countries, driving is done on the right hand side of the road while in the United Kingdom it is on the left hand side. What happens when a well-meaning, African immigrant comes into the United Kingdom, hires or buys a car and drives on the right hand side of the road? He is likely to be involved in an accident which will clearly be his fault. It is possible that there would be casualties, despite his squeaky clean record before coming to the United Kingdom. He would have acted sincerely, but would have been sincerely wrong. He is likely to be convicted for dangerous driving and a plea of ignorance to prevent a conviction will not hold sway in the courts. If you must drive in a country, you must know the laws of driving in that country.

Many Africans driving in the United Kingdom today may not have heard of the term pelican crossing or seen many other unfamiliar road signs before they came to the United Kingdom. They however soon realised that they had to know these terms, what they stood for and how to apply them in the right circumstance if they wanted to pass their driving test, as well as obtain and retain their licence. There have also been couples from the United Kingdom who holiday in certain countries unaware that in those places, open displays of affection, such as kissing in public are not permitted there. They did so at their peril and were charged with acts they never thought were illegal.

Similarly, if you must raise children in the United Kingdom, you must familiarise yourself with at least some aspects of the law relating to children and families in the United Kingdom. As will be discussed further in this book, many well-meaning parents have not done so to their own detriment with on occasion, devastating effects on the whole family. Ignorance of the law is never an excuse and indeed, "the laws in the United Kingdom are not very nice when you fall foul of them." I will highlight a few salient areas and points of law you need to be familiar with in relation to child welfare and protection.

Be warned! This chapter and the next may appear intellectual; however the content is very important to this book.

The Children Act 1989 (CA 1989)

This is the major comprehensive code of law governing the care and upbringing of children in the United Kingdom. It has a wide ambit covering both the private and public law relating to the care and upbringing of children and the provision of services to them and their families. The aim is always to promote the best possible outcome and future for the child.

The Act is divided into sections with sections 17 and 47 being the most significant in regards to public authority intervention in private family life. Sections 17 and 47 define and highlight when a child should be deemed as being, 'in need' and 'at risk of significant harm' respectively and the services that should be provided to such children.

A child is defined as being a child 'in need' in Section 17, if they are unlikely to achieve or maintain, or have the opportunity of achieving, or maintaining, a reasonable standard of health or development without the provision for them of services by a local authority. The section also applies where their health or development is likely to be significantly impaired or further impaired, without the provision of such services, or if the children are disabled. It is generally expected that local authorities and others with a professional concern for children will undertake this general duty wherever possible through voluntary arrangements with parents and their children.

Section 47 places a duty on local authorities to investigate a child's welfare when either emergency protection measures have been taken or there is reasonable cause to suspect that a child is suffering or is likely to suffer significant harm. The investigation must involve any necessary enquiries to enable the local authority to decide whether they should take any action to safeguard or promote the child's welfare. The CA 1989 is supported by subsequent legislation such as those referred to below.

The Children Act 2004 (CA 2004)

This does not replace or duplicate the CA 1989. The Government's response after the Victoria Climbie Enquiry (see pages 111/112) led to child protection reforms including the Every Child Matters agenda and the 2004 Act. This Act basically changes the structure within which services for children are delivered.

The aim is to focus services more effectively around the needs of children, young people and their families. In particular, the Act places a duty on local authorities to make arrangements whereby key agencies and organisations cooperate to improve the wellbeing of children. It places a huge emphasis on all childcare professionals working together and on early intervention to promote the child's welfare. The Act states that safeguarding and promoting a child's welfare is everyone's responsibility and should be encouraged so that the need for compulsory action (for example, using police protection powers or court orders to remove children from their parents) to protect children from harm is reduced.

The European Convention on Human Rights (ECHR) / Human Rights Act (HRA) 1998

The Convention for the Protection of Human Rights and Fundamental Freedoms (commonly known as the European Convention on Human Rights (ECHR) is an international treaty to protect human rights and fundamental freedoms in Europe and it came into force in 1953. Some of the most important provisions of the Act in relation to children's welfare include Articles 3, 5, 6 and 8.

Individuals are entitled to take their complaints to the European Court of Human Rights in Strasbourg. The ECHR was incorporated into English domestic law by the Human Rights Act 1998 (HRA). The HRA 1998 now makes available in the United Kingdom courts a remedy where any breach of a convention right occurs, without the need to go to the European Court of Human Rights in Strasbourg.

Article 3 states that 'no one should be subjected to torture or to inhuman or degrading treatment or punishment.'

Article 5 states that, 'everyone has the right to liberty and no one shall be deprived of his liberty' except in certain circumstances and the section continues by outlining these instances.

Article 6 states the right to a fair hearing and Article 8 states the right of 'respect for private and family life, his home and his correspondence' and continues of course, with exceptions to the rule.

The United Nations Convention on the Rights of the Child 1989 (UNCRC)

The United Kingdom is a party to this Convention. The Convention upholds the principles that children have human rights, are psychological beings and that the development of child protection systems in the countries that are party to the Convention are central to the United Nations Convention on the Rights of the Child (UNCRC). The UNCRC defines children's rights as consisting of *protection*, *participation* and *provision*. These include the rights to be protected from any form of maltreatment or exploitation, to participate in decisions and actions that affect them and the right to have the provision of education and other basic needs met. Children's rights also include the duty of the state to support parents and families.

Key Concepts under the Children Act 1989
The Child

The Children Act 1989, case law and local authorities define and accept a child as anyone who has not yet reached their 18th birthday with exceptions for children with disabilities in certain circumstances. A child in many instances also includes an unborn child after about *26 weeks' gestation period but before the actual birth*. Steps can therefore be taken to protect an unborn child by law at that stage if it is considered that the parents are putting the child at risk of significant harm through their behaviour. This is usually done through pre-birth assessments and pre-birth conferences by local authorities' children services to prepare to safeguard the particular child at birth.

The ages of 16 to 18 remain a grey area in clearly distinguishing who a child is in the United Kingdom. For example, a 16 year old can get married, but cannot drive a car or vote in elections. A 16 year old can work and live independently as an adult, his status as a child however does not change or prevent his entitlement to services or protection. Also the fact that a child lives with his parents does not mean he gains his legal identity and status as a person from them. In other words, the parents do not own the child. The child is a completely separate legal entity from his parents and someone with separate rights recognised by law and the system. That is why in issues relating to the child, the law of the land and not the parents, will always have the final say. The local authority where each child lives is usually ultimately responsible for safeguarding and promoting that child's welfare.

Looked-After Children (LAC)

Where a child cannot be cared for by his birth parents and family and comes into local authority care with or without their consent or has to be removed from his birth family and placed in public care compulsorily, the child will become what is known as a Looked-After Child or LAC. It is a general term introduced by the CA 1989. It covers all children who are accommodated, detained or in care of a local authority. The children may be in a variety of placements including foster care, residential care or residential schools.

Paramountcy Principle

The CA 1989 directs the court to treat the welfare of the child in all matters concerning him as the *paramount consideration*. In other words, when the parents and the child's rights conflict, it is the child's interest and wellbeing that will usually be the first, supreme and overriding consideration. This approach has also been transferred to other areas of practice in relation to children and their families and not just within the court arena.

CASE 4 - PARAMOUNTCY PRINCIPLE

Mr Braimoh was a widower and therefore a single parent to his three children aged 4, 6, and 8. He worked hard to take care of them but suffered a significant mental health breakdown two years after his wife's death. His local authority children services proposed to remove the children from him as it was deemed that his care of them was no longer good enough, even with the provision of support services. His lawyers argued that removing the children would cause a further deterioration in Mr Braimoh's mental health and he would be more stable if the children remained with him. The court agreed with the evidence that Mr Braimoh's mental health was likely to deteriorate further if the children were removed. The court however concluded that the children's needs and care had to be 'paramount'. They were removed in spite of the effect it may subsequently have had on Mr Braimoh.

Parental Responsibility (PR)

The introduction of this new concept in the CA 1989 is crucial and replaced any previous law pertaining to parental rights and duties. The purpose is;

> *To emphasise the practical reality that bringing up children is a serious responsibility, rather than a matter of legal rights for the parents.*

Parental responsibility covers all the parents' duties towards the child, with their concomitant powers and authority over the child, together with some procedural rights for protection against interference. It represents the fundamental status of parents. It is therefore important to remember that any rights parents have are embedded within their PR.

A mother automatically has PR for her child from birth. However, the father will only have it automatically if he was married to the mother at the time of the child's birth or from the 1st December 2003, if both parents jointly registered the birth of the child and the father is named on the birth certificate. A father can also obtain this by entering into a parental responsibility agreement with the mother, by means of a parental responsibility order from a court and/or by marrying the mother of the child. *Living with the mother, even for a long time does not give a father automatic PR.*

The above provision is contrary to the practice in many areas of the African continent where the father of a child usually assumes the cultural, financial and sometimes legal right of PR for the child.

What Does Parental Responsibility Entail?

The law does not define this in its entirety, but it generally includes: providing a home for the child, having contact with and living with the child, protecting and maintaining the child, disciplining the child, choosing and providing for the child's education, determining the religion of the child, agreeing to the child's medical treatment, naming the child and agreeing to any change of the child's name, accompanying the child outside the United Kingdom and agreeing to the child's emigration, should the issue arise, being responsible for the child's property, appointing a guardian for the child, and if necessary, allowing confidential information about the child to be disclosed.

CASE 5 - PARENTAL RESPONSIBILITY

Sibongile and Jabu came from South Africa and lived together in the United Kingdom for twelve years although they never married. They broke up six months ago and their children, 11 year old Abrianna and 6 year old Tania spend five days a week with Jabu, as Sibongile is an air stewardess who is frequently out of the country. When Abrianna needed an eye operation and he had to fill some forms, Jabu was shocked to discover that he only had parental responsibility and the connected rights with regard solely to Tania, and not Abrianna. The hospital insisted on obtaining Sibongile's consent before the operation could go ahead. Abrianna was born before 2003 which means only Sibongile has automatic parental responsibility although Sibongile and Jabu had jointly registered Abrianna's birth and Jabu was named on Abrianna's birth certificate as her father when she was born in 2001. Sibongile and Jabu's relationship has become increasingly acrimonious since their break-up and Jabu now has to apply to the courts to have equal parental responsibility over Abrianna as does Sibongile.

PR for a child may not be an issue that African parents consider on a day to day basis, but this usually becomes important when crucial decisions have to be made on behalf of a child and there is disagreement between the parents, or where authorities refuse to recognise one of the parents as having responsibility, such as in the case above.

Residence Order (RO) and Contact Order (CO)

A Residence order (RO) is an order determining where a child should live. A Contact order (CO) gives a person rights to have regular access to a child as determined by the court.

It is usually best for parents to resolve issues regarding their children amicably through discussion and agreement after a separation or divorce. However, where a legal dispute exists between parents about who a child should live with and how much contact the child has with the absent parent, the court decides this according to the child's welfare and best interests. Sometimes RO is shared between the parents by the courts. On occasion, for example, where the father does not have PR and does not wish to pursue this or a RO, the court can grant a CO determining how often, when and where he can see the child.

As discussed earlier, the child's welfare is always the court's paramount consideration when looking at questions of contact and residence. The court has a duty to consider certain welfare issues such as: the wishes and feelings of the child concerned, their physical, emotional and educational needs, the likely effect of any change in the child's circumstances, the child's age, gender, background and characteristics, any harm or risk of harm and the capability of either or both parents to meet the child's needs.

When an RO is in force, the person in whose favour it has been made can take the child outside the country for up to a month at a time without needing the permission of any other person(s) who has PR. Wider family members, such as grandparents, can also apply for a RO where one or both of the parents are unwilling or unable to care for the child. The RO is also a way of providing someone who is not a birth parent (namely, grandparents and step-parents) with PR and the corresponding rights.

Wishes and Feelings of the Child

The 1989 CA recognises the importance of ascertaining and taking into account the child's own wishes and feelings to an extent commensurate with his age and understanding. This is particularly important in light of the decision in a case now popularly referred to as *Gillick or Frasier competent.*

This was a case brought before the court in which it was decided that a child under the age of 16 could ask for and be given medical treatment in cases where it was determined that the child had sufficient understanding to make such decisions without his parents' permission. Children who are deemed *Gillick competent* can also prevent their parents having access to information on their medical records.

CASE 6 - THE GILLICK DECISION

The Gillick case involved a health department circular advising doctors on the prescription of contraception to minors. The circular stated that the prescription of contraception was a matter for the doctor's discretion, and that they could be prescribed to those less than 16 years of age without parental consent.

Mrs Victoria Gillick, an activist, ran a vigorous campaign against the policy and the matter was subsequently litigated. Mrs Gillick sought a declaration from the court that prescribing contraception to those less than 16 years of age was illegal because the doctor would commit the offence of encouraging sex with a minor, and that it would amount to treatment without consent as consent was a right vested in the parent.

The court held that parental rights did not exist, other than to safeguard the best interests of a minor; that in some circumstances a minor could consent to treatment, and that in these circumstances a parent had no power to prevent treatment or override the minor's wishes.

Lord Scarman proposed that a child could consent if he fully understood the medical treatment being recommended, stating:

"As a matter of law the parental right to determine whether or not their minor child below the age of 16 will have medical treatment terminates if and when the child achieves sufficient understanding and intelligence to understand fully what is proposed."

The ruling holds particularly important repercussions for the legal rights of minor children in England and Wales. It shows clearly that parents do not have absolute authority to make decisions for their minor children. Their authority diminishes with the child's evolving maturity; except in situations that are regulated otherwise by statute (such as getting married). The right to make a decision on any particular matter concerning the child *moves gradually from the parent to the child as the child matures in his pre-teen and teenage years* and becomes increasingly capable of making up his own mind on the matter requiring a decision.

This concept is regularly applied in other areas of child welfare practice. For example, the wishes and feelings of a child less than 16 years of age will be taken into account by local authorities in meeting the needs of that child should he be in public care or of those children for whom they provide a service and work with on occasion without consent from the parents. Attempts are usually made to encourage parental participation in decision-making and to ensure the decision made is commensurate with the particular child's age and level of understanding of the issues concerned.

Most African parents would consider it sacrilegious and offensive for their children to receive any kind of treatment without their knowledge and approval especially while the child lives within their household. It is however the law in the United Kingdom and it can be applied, provided it is in line with the child's wishes. It is therefore advisable that parents develop the type of relationship with their children where the children will not think that sharing this sort of information with the parents will be detrimental to their wellbeing or jeopardise the parent-child relationship.

African Charter on the Rights and Welfare of the Child (ACRWC) or (Children's Charter)

This is an African instrument and the United Kingdom is not a party to this Charter. Its provisions are therefore not applicable in the United Kingdom. I have included it to highlight an interesting observation as this relates to Africans.

This Charter was adopted by the Organisation of African Unity (OAU) in 1990 and brought into force in 1999. In 2001, the OAU legally became the African Union. Like the United Nations Convention on the Rights of the Child (UNCRC), the Children's Charter is a comprehensive instrument that sets out rights and defines universal principles and norms for the status of children. The ACRWC and the UNCRC are the only international and regional human rights treaties that cover the whole spectrum of civil, political, economic, social and cultural rights.

What is interesting is a significant article on which the two pieces of legislation differ - which is the *responsibility* of the child highlighted in Article 31 of the African Children's Charter below.

Article 31: Responsibilities of the Child

Every child shall have responsibilities towards his family and society, the State and other legally recognised communities and the international community. The child, subject to his age and ability, and such limitations as may be contained in the present Charter, shall have the duty;

a) to work for the cohesion of the family, to respect his parents, superiors and elders at all times and to assist them in case of need;
b) to serve his national community by placing his physical and intellectual abilities at its service;
c) to preserve and strengthen social and national solidarity;
d) to preserve and strengthen African cultural values in his relations with other members of the society, in the spirit

of tolerance, dialogue and consultation and to contribute to the moral wellbeing of society;

e) to preserve and strengthen the independence and the integrity of his country;

f) to contribute to the best of his abilities, at all times and at all levels, to the promotion and achievement of African unity.

I added the above to show you how powerful the influence of culture and values can be, even on our laws. The child in the United Kingdom does not have corresponding responsibility by law as obtains in Africa. Some of the areas in the article above could be deemed onerous, abusive and exploitative in practice without the proviso *subject to the child's age and ability*. It is also unclear what local guidance and resources are in place in many parts of Africa to measure how this works in practice, which leaves it open to various interpretations in the different countries where the Charter applies.

Balancing Rights and Responsibilities

It is important however, that rights and responsibilities be well balanced and should be deemed opposite sides of the same coin. One should not exist without the other, even for children, of course, *subject to the child's age and ability*. If a child has a right to education, he should have the corresponding responsibility or duty of attending school.

You will perhaps observe that several indigenous (middle class) families in the United Kingdom tend to incorporate some responsibility and duty values in raising their children. It is highly likely, that Prince Charles and his son, Prince William (although in a different social class) were taught and knew from a very young age the responsibilities and duties that were upon them and walked in that consciousness as they grew up.

Children need to develop a sense of responsibility as they grow up and incorporating appropriate values in this area should be a significant part of every decent child's upbringing. Responsibility instils in children a sense of pride, purpose and strength that cannot be gained in any other way and prevents them from becoming spoilt and thinking the world revolves around them. It is therefore wise that as African parents raise their children in the United Kingdom, they carefully and wisely, weave and merge into their children a consciousness of their rights and some corresponding responsibilities. This way they will be raising a strong and purposeful next generation.

It is however important to remember that the law recognises that children are not the property of their parents to do with as they please. They are individuals in their own right and individuals who need to be valued, nurtured and respected.

CHAPTER 4

Child Abuse

C hild abuse is a highly complex issue which is not easily defined or measured internationally. Child abuse is in many ways a socially defined concept and has changed significantly in definition over the years in almost all societies. What is considered abusive in the United Kingdom has also altered with time and what is viewed as abusive in one society today is not necessarily seen as such in another. The cultural context within which behaviour takes place and the meanings attributed to it by those sharing that culture are important factors to be considered when labelling certain acts as abusive.

For example, many cultures believe a baby or young child should share a bed with its mother and that not doing so shows a lack of care, whilst some other cultures would deem this inappropriate, wrong or even dangerous.

There are many practices which have been proven over the years to be sexually, emotionally, physically and psychologically abusive to children whether it has a cultural basis or not.

This should however not prevent adoption of similar standards in determining what child abuse is. Fortunately,

AFRICAN PARENTS MUST KNOW

people all over the world are now beginning to agree on what is considered harmful and detrimental to a child's wellbeing. There are many practices which have been proven over the years to be sexually, emotionally, physically and psychologically abusive to children whether it has a cultural basis or not. Some of them will be discussed in this book. More and more governments are being urged and pressurised into accepting universal views on major aspects of child abuse and protection of children.

Child Abuse in the United Kingdom: So, what is child abuse in the United Kingdom?

Simply put, it is any form of maltreatment of a child by inflicting harm or failing to act to prevent harm. There are currently five recognised forms of abuse in the United Kingdom - physical, emotional, sexual, neglect and domestic violence. Domestic violence is actually a form of emotional abuse, but this has been discussed separately for ease of reference.

Physical Abuse

Physical abuse is causing direct harm to a child's body. It includes cutting, hitting, shaking, throwing, poisoning, burning or scalding, drowning, force-feeding, suffocating, or otherwise causing physical harm to a child. Department for Children, Schools and Families (DCSF2010).

Female Genital Mutilation (FGM): Also known as female genital cutting or female circumcision is perhaps one of the most grievous forms of physical abuse which thankfully, is decreasing with awareness, but is still accepted as a cultural practice to varying degrees, in many African countries and other parts of the world. It is estimated that about three million girls mostly under the age of 15 undergo the procedure every year in Africa.

Some African groups and other communities have been known to continue the practice in the United Kingdom. According to an article in *The Observer* of 25th July 2010, there is a possibility that between 500 and 2,000 British girls of African and other origins have the procedure carried out on them both in the United Kingdom and abroad, especially during the school summer holidays.

There are different types of FGMs depending on the area or community where it is practised. It constitutes partial or total removal of the external female genitalia or injury to the area. FGM is dangerous to health and medically unnecessary. The short term problems include scarring, severe pain, difficulty in passing urine, infection, bleeding and even death. Longer term problems include difficult and painful sex and childbirth, recurring infections leading to infertility, depression and post-traumatic stress disorder.

It is an offence to take a child out of the United Kingdom for that purpose or to arrange for the procedure to take place. FGM is a serious crime in the United Kingdom. The Female Genital Mutilation Act 2003, makes it illegal for FGM to be performed anywhere in the world on United Kingdom permanent residents of any age and carries a maximum sentence of fourteen years' imprisonment.

CASE 7 - FEMALE GENITAL MUTILATION
RASHIDA'S STORY

"I was looking forward to going on holiday to Mogadishu with my parents in the school summer holidays fourteen years ago, having lived in the United Kingdom all my life. I had been there before, but couldn't remember the last time we went as I was a toddler then and only had pictures to show for that first trip.

That summer fourteen years ago was different. I was coming up for my 12th birthday. My mother had already told me we were going on holiday and I was going to be cut when I got there. I wasn't perturbed. As far as I was concerned, if it was what every girl did, it was fine. It did not sound like a big deal. I was more focused on having a nice time in the sun and meeting members of my family I had only heard about or spoken to over the phone. It did not make too much of a difference that my father and brother Azeez changed their minds at the last minute and only I and my mother went. I was looking forward to having a nice time with or without them.

We arrived at my uncle's lovely house and were warmly welcomed by family members, many of whom I didn't know. The first two days were peaceful and quiet with all of us, mostly females enjoying the lovely sunshine. I still remember sitting outside in the sun under a big tree talking to my aunts and cousins. My mother reminded me that evening that tomorrow was 'the day'. I still remember a couple of my female cousins who were slightly older than me sniggering about the fact that I wasn't yet cut, so I suppose I was anticipating the experience in a strange kind of way.

We went to bed as usual, but I remember being woken up at an earlier time than usual. We were told the cutter had arrived. She seemed a nice enough elderly woman in her sixties. There were also three female family members and a maid, all prepared to help my mother with my cutting. Actually, they came to help hold me down.

I remember the pain like it was yesterday. It was excruciating and I think I passed out as I can only recall waking up to seeing that everyone was gone apart from my mother, an aunt and the maid. When I woke up my mother was stroking my hair, I couldn't walk as my legs had been tied together. Passing urine was agony with the worst pain you can ever imagine. My life has not been the same since then.

I later discovered that I had a really bad circumcision with practically all of my female genitalia removed. I felt strange after I came back to the United Kingdom and I knew that whole process affected me psychologically and mentally. I was no longer the happy-go-lucky fun girl I had been. I felt strangely detached, not only from my body but from everyone and everything around me. I went through a deep period of depression that I still have bouts of.

I am a different person now - I feel like a shell - a significant part of me does not exist anymore. I met my husband three years ago and he is a really lovely man from my country who had also grown up in the United Kingdom. He wept when he found out I was circumcised on our honeymoon. I was surprised as I thought this was what all men wanted - a circumcised virgin. His mother had told him, he said, but he didn't realise it was so bad. My husband has supported me in having some corrective surgery and swears we will never circumcise any of our female children. I love my husband very much and he is a very nice man, but sex continues to be sometimes painful, meaningless and definitely holds no pleasure for me."

FGM is recognised internationally as a violation of the human rights of girls and women. It reflects deep-rooted inequality between the sexes, and constitutes an extreme form of discrimination against women. It is nearly always carried out on minors and is a violation of the rights of children.

The practice also violates a person's right to health, security and physical integrity, the right to be free from torture and cruel inhumane or degrading treatment, and the right to life when the procedure results in death. It is important to alert the relevant authorities if you are concerned that a child resident in the United Kingdom may have the procedure carried out on her in the United Kingdom or abroad. See the resource section at the end of this book for organisations that safeguard children.

Corporal Punishment: Other forms of physical abusive behaviours are mostly related to the discipline and punishment of children for what is perceived as bad behaviour. These include asking a child to raise his hands, carry heavy weights or kneel for long periods of time as well as hitting with a cane, stick or belt. It could also comprise putting pepper in the eyes and genitals, slapping across the face and head, and twisting or pulling of the ears; this list is not exhaustive. The use of the cane was acceptable in schools in the United Kingdom until the 1980s. It has since been completely banned in all schools.

There have however been several reports in recent years that teachers in Islamic schools in the United Kingdom still use this method of discipline frequently. According to the British Broadcasting Corporation (BBC) News on the 18th of October 2011, Britain's *madrassas* (Islamic schools) have faced more than 400 allegations of physical abuse in the past three years. Children as young as 6 years old have reported abuse and parents are said to be under cultural and religious pressure not to report the abuse or press charges. It is likely that actual incidences are much higher than the number recorded if many parents are under cultural or religious pressure to keep silent.

Parents can still 'get away' with some form of corporal punishment by 'chastising' their children 'reasonably' in the United Kingdom. The concept of significant harm in the Children Act 1989 is therefore the only guidance as to when any of these behaviours is considered serious enough to warrant protective intervention by the local authority where the child resides. The seriousness of an isolated incident of physical abuse or frequency of several minor ones plays a part in determining if abuse has occurred.

Significant Harm: The Children Act 1989 introduced the concept of significant harm as the threshold that justifies compulsory intervention in family life in the best interests of children, and gives local authorities a duty to make enquiries to decide whether they should take action to safeguard or promote the welfare of a child who is suffering, or likely to suffer, significant harm.

There are no absolute criteria on which to rely when judging what constitutes significant harm. Consideration of the severity of ill-treatment may include the degree and the extent of physical harm, the duration and frequency of abuse and neglect, the extent of pre-meditation, and the presence or degree of threat, coercion, sadism and bizarre or unusual elements (DCSF 2010). It is important to remember that what is common practice in some parts of Africa, may be deemed unacceptable in the United Kingdom. I will explain how this may work in practice.

Defence of Reasonable Punishment

Simply put, hitting or smacking a child is an assault and therefore a crime in the United Kingdom. Section 58 of the CA 2004 however allows for a defence of reasonable punishment where the child has not suffered physical injury or suffered what may be considered as acts of cruelty.

For example, it would be wrong to hit a member of the public, and you would be deemed to have committed an assault if you do. You can argue the reason of self-defence if you can prove that you hit the other person in order to prevent that person from harming you. This may not however prevent you from being charged or arrested for the offence in the first instance.

... the defence of 'reasonable punishment' will also not prevent the situation being assessed or investigated when an initial concern is brought to the attention of the authorities.

This is similar to the law on reasonable punishment which has been considered ambiguous and confusing by many professionals. The question is; is it acceptable to hit a child in the United Kingdom? The answer is no. You will however not be charged or convicted for doing so, if your action is considered reasonable punishment. Smacking is therefore still indirectly permissible in the United Kingdom as long as the action of the parent is deemed 'reasonable'.

It is important to note that the defence of reasonable punishment of a child does not exist in other European countries and there is pressure on the United Kingdom to remove this defence from its laws completely. The United Kingdom nonetheless retains this, thereby giving parents an indirect right to smack their children. It is however important to note that it will <u>not</u> be deemed reasonable punishment where an implement had been used or the child has been left with a visible mark or appears justifiably, overly emotionally distressed by the punishment. The use of the defence of reasonable punishment will also not prevent the situation being assessed or investigated when an initial concern is brought to the attention of the authorities.

What is likely to happen in practice?

Several local authorities in the United Kingdom differ on how the law and the procedures are interpreted and implemented to varying degrees. Several factors will affect the threshold for intervention, but more and more situations are likely to be reacted to as follows: if a child reports or discloses physical chastisement or is observed by other persons to have an injury which does not appear accidental, the child's circumstance is likely to be reported to the local authority's children social services and investigated by social services alone or in conjunction with the police as *a child likely to have suffered significant harm* (sec 47 CA 1989) or at least assessed by social services *as a child in need* (sec 17 CA 1989) depending on the severity of the initial information received and any subsequent information gathered.

Section 17 Assessments under the 1989 Children Act mean that the circumstances of the child will be addressed through the gathering and analysing of information known as an initial or core assessment.

The initial assessment is a framework for social workers to gather and analyse information on the child's circumstances within a seven-day period.

A core assessment provides a structured, in-depth assessment of a child or young person's needs where their circumstances are complex. The core assessment provides a structured framework for social workers to record information gathered from a variety of sources to provide evidence for their professional judgment, facilitate analysis, decision-making and planning. A core assessment should be completed within thirty-five working days of its commencement. A completed core assessment record is then used to develop the plan for the child or young person. Assessments are usually carried out with parental consent.

A section 47 investigation means that social services must carry out an investigation when they have reasonable cause to believe that a child living in their area has suffered or is likely to suffer significant harm. The purpose of this

> *Section 47 investigations are carried out regardless of parental approval or consent.*

investigation is to ascertain if a crime has been committed against a child and to decide what should be done to safeguard and promote the child's welfare.

Section 47 investigations are usually carried out by social services and the Child Abuse Investigation Team (CAIT) of the Police Force. There are, however, situations where the police withdraw from the investigations and further assessments are continued by the local authority children social services as a single agency. This is usually when there is insufficient evidence that a crime has been committed against the child. Section 47 investigations are carried out regardless of parental approval or consent. Although consent is usually sought from parents if there is a need for a medical examination of a young child; consent can be sought from the courts if parents refuse.

The child's family will be visited and his parents will be asked questions to clarify the reported incident against the child and to help the workers understand the family situation better. If it is considered at the initial stage that the child has not suffered significant harm, it is likely that an initial or core assessment of the child's welfare will be completed by the social services department alone, with the aim of understanding the child's needs and circumstances better, and to provide the family with appropriate information, advice and/or support.

If the child is deemed to have suffered significant harm and is likely to continue doing so, the child may be removed from his parents under police-protection powers for up to seventy-two hours as a result of a Section 47 investigation. The local authority may ask the parents to agree to the child being accommodated for a longer period to complete their investigations. Section 20 of the Act makes provisions for this and states that;

> A local authority may provide accommodation for
> any child within their area if they consider that
> to do so would safeguard or promote the child's
> welfare.

Alternatively, the local authority will have to apply to the courts for an order to protect the child for a longer period if the parents do not agree.

Remember that it is likely to be considered a crime of assault and physical abuse against a child where an implement has been used, the child has suffered actual injury such as cuts, bruises or where the child has described clear and credible accounts of cruel punishments such as those described above. Other factors which will be considered in determining whether abuse has taken place will include the intention of the perpetrator, age of the child, the context and other risk elements such as previous incidents, the vulnerability of the child and his past and current relationship with the perpetrator.

If a child is deemed to have suffered, or is likely to suffer significant harm in the future, he will be placed on a *Child Protection Plan* if he returns to or remains at home with his parents. This means that the local authority and partner agencies will devise a plan and each agency will play a role in safeguarding and promoting the child's welfare and supporting the family.

There are however instances where it is considered not in the child's best interests to return to the parents. If the parents are not in agreement with the decision, the local authority will have to initiate *care proceedings* which is the legal process whereby the court is asked whether a child should go into local authority care or not.

In determining whether a child has been abused or a crime has been committed against a child, much depends on the discretion and professional judgement of the police and social workers, the evidence before them, their judgment as to what is reasonable and what is best for the child, and all the other surrounding factors, such as the circumstance of the parents, the likelihood of the parents changing their style of parenting and the child's wishes and feelings. If the case goes to court, the defence of reasonable punishment is unlikely to hold sway if there is evidence of actual or grievous bodily harm, such as bruising and cuts.

The process of investigation and assessment can be a very daunting and traumatic experience for African families who have had no previous dealings with the police or children social services and have no idea of how the child protection system in the United Kingdom works. It is therefore always advisable to seek independent legal advice and support during the whole process. The Family Rights Group (FRG) is a voluntary organisation that provides advice to families whose children are involved with children's social care services because of welfare needs or concerns. See the resource section for the organisation's details.

Impact of Culture

It is important to mention at this stage, that on occasion, the intentions of many African parents have been grossly misunderstood often due to their inappropriate or colloquial use of the English language which may convey a completely different meaning to non-Africans. For example, using the words, "I beat her" or the child saying, "He beats me" will convey a strong message of the child suffering a higher degree of harm than the words "I smacked her" or "He smacks me". The use of any implement, however lightly used suggests abuse. It is also not uncommon for many Africans to speak very fast in loud voices with many gesticulations when distressed and agitated, which non-Africans may also misinterpret as aggressive or threatening behaviour.

Some otherwise well-meaning parents bring up their children with strict rules, punishing and smacking often, believing this is the way to keep the children on the straight and narrow. Unfortunately, as the years go by, they have to punish and smack harder to get the desired effect and end up with either a rebellious or defiant child who eventually stands up to them, or the fearful, abused child with low self-esteem who cannot stand up for himself.

Many well-meaning parents have also ended up receiving police cautions, convictions and serving prison sentences for the physical abuse of their children, while the parents sincerely believed they were only being strict 'no-nonsense,' 'zero-tolerance' parents disciplining their child. Many have also suffered family breakdowns and lost their children to the care system of local authorities.

Several are just completely unaware of the law and the prevalent culture in the United Kingdom and only find out after they have got themselves into trouble with the law.

CASE 8 - CORPORAL PUNISHMENT

Andrew Mugadza previously worked as an accountant under an oppressive government in his home country. He re-trained as a nurse in the early 1990s when he came to the United Kingdom. He met his wife, Barbara, who is also a nurse, during his training and they now have three children - Daniel, 15; Florah, 14; and Sylvia, 12.

Like many teenagers, Daniel pushed boundaries. He could be moody, stroppy and rude, especially to his parents. Over the past year, he would often talk back to them and refuse to stick to his curfew times. Recently, he has been refusing to participate in household chores.

His father, Andrew, did not believe children had any right to answer their parents back and was becoming increasingly fed up with Daniel's lateness, moodiness, back-chatting and laziness. Daniel's mother, Barbara, believed it was best to coax him to do chores when possible and ignore him when he came in late. Andrew does not agree with Barbara's style of parenting and is of the view that she spoils Daniel and it is one of the reasons why he misbehaves.

Andrew desperately wants his three children, to be happy, grateful and compliant, as in his view, he worked hard to give them all they needed. He did not have major problems with the girls, but Daniel in Andrew's view was getting out of hand. They appeared to be an average family with their problems in private and in the background, until one Friday morning during a school half-term break.

Daniel did not take the bins out the night before, the rubbish collectors were arriving soon and he was refusing to get up, having slept so late. He reluctantly got up after Andrew had shouted at him for about half an hour and threatened to, throw him out of the house.

On his way out of the front door, Andrew had called Daniel an idiot. Daniel mumbled some words, but his reply was still audible, "it takes one to know one" he said. Andrew went after Daniel and slapped him hard across the face. Daniel swung his arm, but Andrew grabbed the arm and slapped Daniel again, pushing him against the wall. Barbara and the girls heard the commotion, came down the stairs, and found Daniel bent over on the floor, crying.

Daniel realised his lip was cut and bleeding and called the police from his mobile phone informing them that he had been assaulted by his father and was bleeding. The police arrived with an ambulance and took Daniel to the hospital. Daniel gave a statement to the police that Andrew, his father had slapped him across the face a few times in the past, and had also struck him with a slipper and a belt. Daniel said his father never hit the girls, as they knew how to comply and keep to the set boundaries.

Daniel was taken into care whilst the case was being investigated. Andrew was arrested and charged. He got off with a community service order but now has a conviction for child cruelty. He remains employed but is unlikely to find it easy to change jobs in the caring profession with that sort of conviction on his record.

Daniel told his social worker he would run away if he were made to return to his parents. Although Andrew is not opposed to Daniel returning home, he refuses to speak to him or his social worker, visit him in his foster placement, or attend any social service meetings regarding him.

The conclusion of Daniel's social worker's assessment is that it was not in Daniel's best interests to return home and he remains in the care of the local authority. Barbara, Florah and Sylvia are distraught and feel torn between the two most important males in their lives.

CASE 9 - CORPORAL PUNISHMENT

Ahmed Potopoto is a leader and a well-respected member of his African community and faith group in the United Kingdom. He was the only surviving child of his parents and had always desired a big family from his youth and being in the United Kingdom was not going to stop him.

Fatmata, his wife, knew this from the time she first met him and they now have eight children - unusual today even for families in their home country. Ahmed took pride in being the breadwinner of his big family. His wife did not work and he provided for all his family's needs from his cab company business.

The size of the family in a four-bedroom end of terrace maisonette meant there had to be proper routines if the house was not to degenerate into chaos. Ahmed secretly loved the noise, the banter and arguments that emanated from the children's rooms but would often keep a stern demeanour as he felt a father should. His favourite role was playing judge or arbiter, settling disputes between the children when one of them came to report the other to him. Abdullah, 14 years old was the eldest, followed by Abubakar, 13; Nimata, 12; Isiaka, 10; Renatu, 8; Ibrahim, 6; Mariam, 3; and the 8-month-old baby, Wahab.

Fatmata had a few friends she met up with sometimes within her faith group, but spent most of her day cleaning, washing, cooking and caring for the baby. She took pride in being a housewife. Her home was always clean and her husband and children were well-fed and taken care of. The couple kept to themselves and had limited association with people and organisations outside their own community and faith group.

Although Ahmed loved his children, physical punishment was his major method of discipline. He believed that a father's words must be few and final. That was how he was raised and he did not know any other way of keeping children on the straight and narrow. He had a couple of helpers - two canes of different sizes kept for that purpose under his bed to carry out his role of family disciplinarian. Abubakar and Abdullah were used to strokes of the cane on the palms of their hands and they took their punishment bravely whenever they stepped out of line. In fact, they just stood with their hands out-stretched, took the strokes 'like a man' and went back to their room.

Nimata was however a different child. She hated being caned so much, she would often scream, shout and cry loudly before her father came near her. On many occasions she had wet herself when she knew 'it' was coming. She had also once attempted to jump out of the bathroom window before her father caught up with her. She knew caning for everyone was going to happen again that evening, as no one had admitted to breaking her father's CD Player and her father had promised to 'deal' with the children if no one admitted to causing the damage when they got back from school.

Nimata, who was usually chatty and loud in class, appeared unhappy and sullen throughout the day. Her teacher noticed and asked her what the matter was. Nimata burst into tears and told her teacher she did not want to go home as she could not 'face it', meaning the physical punishment from her father. Eventually, her teacher calmed her down and called the children social service.

Fatmata, being the available parent at home, was informed of Nimata's disclosure and Nimata was visited at school by a social worker and a police child protection officer. Nimata reported the beatings she and her siblings received from their father on a regular basis. In her statement she said the beatings were fortnightly. Her brothers' view was that it was about once a month or longer, but they all agreed it was with the cane. Abubakar and Abdullah still had a couple of fading old marks around their arms where the cane had struck them on a couple of occasions.

Ahmed Potopoto was surprised to see the police and social workers on his doorstep as he came in from work. He admitted to physically hitting all his children to varying degrees according to their age as his main form of discipline and showed the police officer and social workers the canes he used. He was shocked when the police took the canes with them and decided to use their protection powers to remove all the children apart from baby Wahab, to a place of safety from where the children were interviewed and investigations into the abuse were carried out. Ahmed looked on quietly as the officers spoke to him but did not hear or understand anything they said apart from, "we will be removing the children from you today to a place of safety."

Fatmata screamed, wailed and shouted, rolling all over the floor and causing a scene in front of the neighbours as the children were ushered into the social workers' and police cars. The seven children who were placed with three different foster carers disclosed physical punishment that was considered harsh and unreasonable in the United Kingdom. The investigation was time-consuming because of the number of children involved and stressful for all parties, and Ahmed became increasingly angry and depressed.

The children were put on a child protection plan (formerly known as the child protection register) under the category of physical abuse after a child protection conference was convened. Ahmed accepted a police caution for child cruelty (he was not even sure what this meant) and the children were eventually returned home with a plan of a fortnightly visit from a social worker as part of the child protection plan.

Ahmed worked from 9am to 7pm during the week and could only be available on a couple of occasions when the social worker could visit late in the evening. The children were taken off the child protection plan after six months due to the fact that other aspects of their needs were well met and they did not report any further instances of physical abuse. Ahmed had also made it clear that he would no longer be hitting the children with a cane. Ahmed was referred to a local parenting group but could only attend once.

> The timing clashed with his working hours and there were no other males there.
>
> Abdullah, Abubakar and Nimata in particular now regularly flaunt Ahmed's rules. Ahmed cannot use the only method of discipline he is comfortable and confident with and now feels completely disempowered as a parent.

Neglect

This is another category of abuse defined in *Working Together to Safeguard Children* as,

> The persistent failure to meet a child's physical or psychological needs, which is likely to result in the serious impairment of the child's health or development.

It may involve a parent failing to provide adequate food, clothing and shelter; failing to protect a child from harm or danger; failing to ensure adequate supervision; failing to provide consistent education; or failing to ensure a child has access to appropriate medical care or treatment.

I must however emphasise that even though the definition uses the term *persistent* failure, one significant act can be deemed to constitute neglect. As in all areas of child abuse, depending on the severity and the available evidence, neglect is a crime for which a parent can be cautioned, charged and even imprisoned. Many parents have been neglectful and charged for example, for failing to ensure their children attend school on a regular basis or for not attending to their health needs. I will discuss two common areas where some parents have been deemed neglectful concerning their children's welfare.

Home Alone: Some parents have been known to leave young children on their own or in the care of slightly older siblings. I mentioned a scenario earlier under isolation/poor social support. When a parent has poor social support and has to go to work, shop, attend community group meetings such as mosques, churches or clubs, there is the temptation to take a risk and do things quickly outside the home without taking the children along.

Parents often take unimaginable and unquantifiable risks when they do this, and there have been children who, in some situations, have woken up frightened and crying having found their parents absent, or worse, children who had choked, started fires and died or been raped or abducted whilst the parents were away. Many children are also fast becoming what are known as *latch-key kids*. This is where a child from a very young age regularly goes home from school or other places on his own, has his own key to enter the house and spends a significant number of hours alone and unsupervised.

In the United Kingdom, there is no legally set age for when your child can be left home alone, but it is an offence to leave a child on their own if it places them at risk. It would be considered neglectful if a child is left unsupervised "in a manner likely to cause unnecessary suffering or injury to health." However, several factors would be considered to determine neglect in this area, these include: the age and maturity of the child, the ability of the child to reach you or others in an emergency, the length of time the child is left unsupervised and the frequency, and if the child is happy and comfortable with the arrangement.

Babies and toddlers *must never* be left on their own, whether in a house, car or shop, and young children under the age of 12 may not be mature enough to cope with an emergency. There is no legal age for when a child can babysit another child or a sibling and each case is usually determined on its merits and by the police and social services using their professional judgment to evaluate each situation they come in contact with.

Children differ from one another in their reliability and maturity, so; gauging an appropriate age to care for siblings when the carer is less than 16 years old can be difficult.

Children differ from one another in their reliability and maturity, so gauging an appropriate age to care for siblings when the carer is less than 16 years old can be difficult. Also, as a child under 16 is not deemed mature enough to live alone by law, it would not be deemed appropriate to leave a child under 16 alone overnight.

CASE 10 - HOME ALONE

Joyce is a single parent of two - Georgina, aged 9 and George, 7. Things were looking good for Joyce as she had recently been granted the right to remain in the United Kingdom with her two children after coming in from Sierra Leone three years ago as an asylum seeker.

Joyce lives in a three-bedroom council property and she had recently got a job as a cleaner at a London Underground Station. The job paid reasonably well; the only problem was the one and a half hour travel time to and from work. The shift hours were 7am to 3pm. The children attended an after-school club, so she was able to pick them up at 5pm.

However, she still had to leave home at 5.30am and faced the dilemma of deciding what to do with the children at that time of the day. Joyce devised a plan of action. She laid the children's clothes out neatly and left their breakfast in the microwave before she left the house. She then called Georgina on the phone from work at 7.30am to get herself and her brother ready for school which was a ten-minute walk away.

Like many young children, 9 year old Georgina did not always fully wake-up from sleep when her mother called. Sometimes she would get up and go straight back to bed; at other times the children would fail to brush their teeth, forget to have breakfast or put on their jackets. There were a few occasions when George had worn his shoes and shirt the wrong way round and refused to comb his hair or let Georgina help him.

Staff at school soon noticed that the children walked to school on their own, turned up late and looked dishevelled on many occasions. The school staff shared their concerns with the local authority's children social services. The police investigation soon revealed that the children had been regularly left at home alone in the mornings for a period of time.

Joyce accepted a caution for neglect and the children were removed from her care for close to two months until the children social service were convinced that she was able to make provisions for their care without leaving them at home alone in the mornings. The leader of her faith group was able to link her with one of their members who was a mature student and in need of accommodation. She offered to move in and care for the children in the mornings in exchange for her lodgings.

Joyce however still has a police caution on her record for child cruelty for neglecting her children and leaving them at risk of harm.

Inadequate Clothing and Food: Several children in the United Kingdom leave home for school every day without being properly fed or clothed and this is not because their parents cannot afford to. Many children are not mature enough to make themselves a healthy breakfast and dress appropriately for school without adult supervision and help. Many children arrive at school cold, hungry and dirty without appropriate shoes and clothing such as warm coats in the winter months. Many others are known to buy crisps and fizzy drinks for breakfast on their way to school.

The long-term effects of this type of neglect include; poor concentration in school, obesity and angry children displaying anti-social behaviour. Poor nutrition affects the behaviour of children, their school performance and their overall development.

Ensuring a child has appropriate clothing and food are basic needs which should always be a priority in parenting and must never be used as a method of discipline or punishment. There are many nutritious breakfast meals that can be prepared in five minutes or less. Most African parents are passionate about their children succeeding academically and must therefore remember that there is a strong correlation between good, nutritious meals and academic achievement.

It is the practice in many families, Africans included, for the younger ones to wear items which have been used by an older child or for siblings to share. There is nothing wrong with this practice as long as the children are fine with it and the items are clean and wearable. Some African parents in the United Kingdom, mostly due to economic reasons, buy clothing or shoes that are more than a size too big for their children so the children can grow into them and get the maximum wear possible from them for many years. Ill-fitting clothes are uncomfortable and shoes that are the wrong size can be damaging to feet. Also, as this is not common practice in the United Kingdom, it is likely to cause any child a great deal of embarrassment and psychological distress amongst his peers. A child is likely to be ostracised or bullied for looking awkward and being even more different than he already is.

Parents should work hard to reduce or eliminate any other disadvantage to their children. As in all other groups, there is a wide variation in income levels among African parents. It is well worth considering buying cheaper clothing for babies, toddlers and younger children who cannot tell the difference as long as they are warm and clean. There are many clothing stores with good quality cheap clothing that can be mixed and matched with more expensive brands. Taking older children to shops with you to get their own clothes and agreeing on what to buy, can also help to prevent you wasting your hard-earned money on items they do not like.

Emotional Abuse

Emotional abuse is the persistent emotional maltreatment of a child such as to cause severe and persistent adverse effects on the child's emotional development. This involves conveying to a child that they are worthless or unloved, inadequate or valued only in so far as they meet the needs of another person. It may include verbally abusing a child, threatening a child, reacting to minor mistakes, constant criticisms and put-downs, not allowing the child to express his or her views, or preventing him from participating in normal activities. Some form of emotional abuse is involved in all types of maltreatment of children although it can also occur alone.

Academic Support or Pressure: Many parents want their children to do well academically and it is important that they are encouraged and supported to do so. There are however concerns that in an attempt to make children excel academically, many parents including Africans, pressurise and push children beyond their ability and capability, making them feel their intrinsic worth is tied to their academic success.

Some parents make their children study from dawn to dusk with no breaks in between, in the hope that this will make them academic geniuses. Some affirm and favour their academically able and bright children to the detriment of the non-academic or poorly-performing ones. The parents are therefore not only emotionally abusing some of their children but also sowing seeds of sibling rivalry. Needless to say, not all children are or will be academically bright. It is important that parents recognise this and affirm the other strengths, gifts and talents in their average or poorly-performing children whilst still encouraging and supporting them to do their best academically.

Many parents grew up on the receiving end of their own parents' critical and sharp tongues and remember how this made them feel. Many parents will also admit they have said something hurtful to their children which they later regret. Some parents however appear oblivious to the impact of threats, extreme criticisms and put-downs on their children, and unfortunately some do this on a regular basis until it becomes a difficult habit to break. Many parents even criticise their children in front of other family members, neighbours and strangers sometimes to portray to others that they are strict, in control and have a firm rein on their children.

Historically, Africans are not known for giving on-going physical affection such as kisses and hugs to children once they are past the toddler years. This is still acceptable in many parts of Africa where families live communally, and there are many caregivers and other culturally acceptable ways of demonstrating emotional care and affection to children.

Some parents feel they must help their children be strong early in life and prepare them for a hostile world, by giving them tough love. Some other parents might even believe that giving or showing too much physical affection, as well as giving praise and attention will actually spoil the child or make him soft or a sissy. The mind-set of many is to train the child in being independent and disciplined. Consideration may not be given to the fact that unkind words coupled with lack of affection in a society where it is the norm, can deflate a child's self-esteem and cause deep wounds that may not heal for many years or even for life.

The only attention some children end up receiving from their parents is negative - which happens when they misbehave. As some negative attention can be better than none at all, this sometimes means that the child unconsciously misbehaves in order to at least receive some attention, whilst the parent can become more emotionally distant and sometimes even abusive in other ways. This can develop into a vicious cycle, which becomes a difficult pattern to break with some parents not being aware or ever reflecting on what is really happening. On occasion, some external or professional help is needed to break this cycle of negativity.

Sexual Abuse

Sexual abuse involves forcing or enticing a child or young person to take part in sexual activities. It does not necessarily have to involve a high level of violence or matter whether or not the child is aware of what is happening. The activities may involve physical contact, including assault by penetration (for example, oral, anal or vaginal sex) or non-penetrative acts such as masturbation, kissing, rubbing and touching outside or inside of clothing.

Sexual abuse of a child may also include non-contact activities, such as involving children in looking at, or in the production of sexual images, watching sexual activities, encouraging children to behave in sexually inappropriate ways, or grooming a child in preparation for abuse (including via the internet). Sexual abuse is mostly, but not solely perpetrated by adult males though women and older children have been known to commit acts of sexual abuse on children.

Many men and women who experience severe or long-term sexual abuse in childhood will develop some form of mental health problems in adulthood. A significant number of child sexual abuse victims will go on to suffer some degree of anxiety, depression and emotional difficulties in relationships. Cases of sexual abuse are seriously under-reported to the police and other services generally, and the situation is likely to be similar in African communities.

Many sexual abuse victims do not even tell the people closest to them.

It is therefore important that parents are aware of the possibility of this sort of abuse and do their best to protect their children both within the home and outside it. You must ensure that any alternative care arrangements you make for your children are suitable and that the children are happy with them. Listen and watch out for subtle cues that your child may be giving out regarding people they have contact with.

Many perpetrators of child sexual abuse are people that are well-known to and trusted by the parents and this may make it even more difficult for the parents to suspect abuse or for the child to disclose it. Some perpetrators are experts at grooming children. They appear kind, give the children gifts and attention and make their child victims feel secure, blurring the boundary lines between appropriate and inappropriate behaviour thereby confusing the child whilst the abuse goes on. The psychological effect of sexual abuse is known to be particularly damaging when the perpetrator is a parent or close family member.

Parents should start teaching their children simple rules about their bodies and personal safety from a very young age. Children should be told clearly that they do not have to do anything they do not want or like with any adult or older child. They should be taught that their bodies and those of others are precious, private and not to be violated by others. It is interesting that one of the first words children learn to say is 'No'. Teach your children to say 'No' to what they do not like.

Build your child's self-esteem with lots of praise, love and attention. Sexual predators and bullies tend to pick on less confident, lonely or neglected children. Your children are more likely to confide in you and tell you things that worry them if they believe you have time for them and will listen to them. Let them know you are never too busy to care or listen to what may be of concern to them.

Domestic Violence (DV)

Domestic violence (DV) is any incident of threatening behaviour, violence or abuse (psychological, physical, sexual, financial or emotional) between adults who are or have been intimate partners or family members. There are occasions when the perpetrator is the female, but it is most prevalent between male perpetrators and female victims.

Children living in households where DV is happening are now identified as being at risk of significant harm. It is considered that a child has suffered significant harm or is at risk from it, when he sees or hears the ill-treatment of another within the household he lives. It is rare to find people talk about DV openly in African communities, and for this reason, it may be assumed that it is not happening or people may convince themselves it is happening only at a very low level. DV is just as common in African communities as it is in other communities and not limited to any socio-economic class, religion or nationality.

There are several factors that can precede DV in African communities. Stress linked to pressures such as discussed in chapter 2 can be significant factors. The perception of women by men is also just as important. In many African cultures women are seen as inferior or unequal to men, and in some cases, on a par with children.

It is rare to find a customary law in Africa that provides for the protection of women from DV. Some African cultures and customary laws still classify the woman as part of the man's property! In the United Kingdom, men and women are considered equals under the law.

It is however sometimes the case that a woman who suffers DV does not have her own income and has her immigration status dependent on her spouse. She may feel trapped and unable to leave the relationship due to a fear of isolation, deportation, destitution and separation from her children and the stigma that accompanies this within her local and wider African community. Africans must be determined to tackle DV within their communities and encourage victims and perpetrators to seek help early.

According to the organisation, Women's Aid, over two women are killed each week in the United Kingdom, by a current or ex-partner. One in four women will experience DV in their lifetime and at least 750,000 children a year witness DV in the United Kingdom. Children can experience both short and long-term cognitive, behavioural and emotional effects as a result of witnessing DV.

Every child exposed to DV will respond differently to the trauma from it. Some children may appear resilient and not exhibit any outward negative effects but this does not mean they have not suffered psychologically. Some of the effects of DV on children include poor concentration, low self-esteem, under-achievement at school, bed-wetting, nightmares, stress and anxiety, violent or aggressive behaviour and worrying when the perpetrator returns home.

There is also a strong link between DV on women and the physical abuse of children, with the probability being that children are more likely to be physically abused when their mother suffers domestic violence from a partner.

What Victims Should Do: It is difficult to give a simplistic answer as each individual and circumstance differ. Many women may have been advised that the violence would stop if they were more submissive or obedient but some have experienced the violence increasing as they have done so. This approach also suggests that the victim can control the violence and places the responsibility on her to do so.

Victims of DV must think of the safety of themselves and their children first. It is important that victims find someone they can talk to and seek prompt and appropriate help. If the intention is to leave the violent partner, it is best to do so in a planned way. Arranging for a place to stay in an unfamiliar area and enrolling children in new schools can be a daunting experience if not planned properly. DV has also been known to escalate on occasion after the victim has left the relationship.

In practice, a mother who is not willing to end her relationship with an abusive partner and put safety measures in place for herself and her children, may be deemed to be exposing her children to violence and placing them at risk of harm.

For many African women, there are countless overlapping complexities to be addressed. Apart from the dependency as well as the threat of deportation or losing her children, there are also cultural implications for the woman. Many have expressed anxiety about their spouse having paid a bride price, which in some African cultures is the seal of an unbreakable covenant or proof of ownership of the woman by the man. Many women also worry about the stigma of separation and divorce and the repercussions from the community of getting the police and other external agencies involved in what most consider a private matter. It is important to remember however, that support is available and many women have been able to overcome these obstacles with the right support.

Support for Perpetrators: DV shows in the perpetrator, a lack of skills in dealing with conflict, anger issues perhaps linked to other underlying factors and usually a need for domination and control in the manner of school ground bullies. Many DV perpetrators are psychologically sick and need professional help. Men and boys should be taught early and made to understand that violence is not the way to resolve conflict. While some men have been able to address and stop their violent behaviour, several others have not. Many others will show remorse and stop for a short period of time, but like addicts of many a bad vice, they start again. Organisations that provide information, advice and support to women experiencing domestic violence and male perpetrators are included in the resource section at the end of this book.

CHAPTER 5

The Trafficked Child

Child-trafficking is the recruitment, transportation, transferring, harbouring, or receiving of children for the purpose of exploitation. Trafficking of children for all kinds of exploitation is worldwide and not peculiar to any culture.

Child-trafficking is made worse in societies where there is no compulsory or properly documented birth registration for all children. Children can therefore go missing without any records to show that they ever even existed. Many children are taken from remote parts of various countries by human traffic traders who act as brokers, sometimes selling them off in the cities of those countries as well as abroad. Trafficked children usually have very little choice in what happens to them and the exploitation they experience takes several forms including sexual exploitation.

The Domestic Servant: The trafficking of children for the purpose of domestic servitude or domestic slavery appears to be the most common form of child-trafficking in African communities in the United Kingdom.

In March 2011, a female church leader was jailed for 11½ years after being found guilty of trafficking children into the United Kingdom for use as domestic slaves at her home in East London. The mother of five is the first person to be jailed for trafficking children into the United Kingdom for domestic servitude. Her offence was bringing two children and a 21 year old woman to the United Kingdom from Africa illegally and using them as servants. She was said to have viciously beaten them when they failed to please her.

At the risk of playing devil's advocate, it is quite possible that she was ignorant of the fact that she was committing a grievous criminal offence as domestic servitude and physical chastisement of children is a fairly common and acceptable practice in many parts of Africa.

Effects of a Class System: There is a clear class system in operation in many African countries and communities. It is not uncommon to have servants live within your household in Africa. In some cases, these servants are either close or distant relatives from the same geographical area, town or region, and their immediate families, stricken by poverty, usually loan them out to more affluent members of their community when they are no longer able to feed, clothe and educate their expanding families. Going to live with a new family who can clothe, feed and in many cases educate them is not only seen as the lesser of two evils, but also as a very positive move. Many recipient families prefer younger children who can be moulded rather than adults who are already set in their ways, as adult servants are also likely to be less compliant.

In many arrangements, the servant's family also receives a regular payment. As there is no minimum wage in most parts of Africa which is commensurate with wages in the United Kingdom, what the servant's family receives is a relatively trivial amount. Usually there is no financial remuneration paid to the child's family when the child servant is being educated by the recipient family. There is an assumption that the education as well as the daily feeding and clothing compensate for the help with domestic chores the child or young person renders in return. There is therefore no need for further financial reward.

The extent to which the recipient family cares for the child will depend on several factors. On occasion, it would depend on how close a relative the child is, how endeared they are to him and how compliant or well-behaved the child servant is. For the most part, these kinds of arrangements are widely practiced and work fairly well in many African societies where the class structure is perpetuated by stark deprivation, a non-existent welfare system and poverty.

Problems arise when some African immigrants come to the United Kingdom and want to continue with similar arrangements due to the pressure of work, childcare duties and the need to be on top of household chores. This practice would however be considered abusive and non-compliant with the law in the United Kingdom.

Illegal Entrance: The first question to arise in such a scenario would be under what circumstance and with what intention was the child who is being used as a domestic servant brought into the United Kingdom?

As is currently being discovered, many of the children are brought in illegally and through fraudulent means. Some are brought in using fake or other people's passports. The passport usually disappears once the child enters the United Kingdom and the child settles within a household.

On some occasions, the children are registered at school, but at other times they are not. Usually, they are expected to carry out similar functions as a servant within the household as they did before coming to the United Kingdom. The hours worked can be long and ad hoc, especially when they do not attend school; there is no contract or scheduled time off.

The arrangement is all very informal in a manner that best suits the recipient of the child. Sometimes the child's family back in Africa continues to receive payment, but in many cases, payments cease. It is however very rare that the children themselves are directly paid and you are then left with a child living in a household in the United Kingdom with no legal status and no pay. In some instances, the carers become attached to the child and develop a degree of emotional warmth and affection which leads to the child being better cared for. The child may be amiable and understand the process of exchange by which he she came to live in the United Kingdom and may accept his or her lot without question.

The problem of the unresolved immigration status however becomes an issue on many levels. What happens when the family travels abroad on holiday for example? The child will be unable to travel with them. If the child is fortunate enough to attend school, what happens when he is required to go on a school trip abroad with school mates? He will be unable to. In many other cases, the trafficked child is presented with emotional and behavioural problems linked to the trauma of separation from all that is familiar to him.

The carers, not recognising or caring about this aspect of the child's needs, resort to firmer and stricter forms of discipline in a bid to make the child behave better. The situation can become emotionally and physically abusive and fits perfectly into the classic scenario of child-trafficking in the United Kingdom.

It needs to be stated quite clearly here that child-trafficking in any form is a crime in the United Kingdom, and is also punishable by imprisonment.

Trafficked Living: In Africa, a child in domestic servitude may not know any better and may accept this as the norm. The child is also likely to get some time off to see his birth family sometimes as the child may still reside in the same country and vicinity.

However, a child who has been trafficked to the United Kingdom for domestic servitude is unlikely to be able to travel to visit his or her own family. If the child is fortunate enough to attend school, he begins to see how different he is from other students. The child gradually becomes aware that a class system operates within the home he lives, and that he is seen to be of a lower class than the family he now lives with. The recipient family on the other hand see the child as privileged, having given the child this 'wonderful' opportunity to live and school in the United Kingdom. The recipient family compares the child's past life to what he now has and may see the child as extremely unappreciative if his attitude is not one of gratitude.

From the perspective of the recipient family, the child-servant is now far removed from the suffering experienced whilst living with his birth family in Africa. It may be true that the child no longer has to travel miles to fetch water from a well, grind pepper manually or sleep on a floor mat in a mosquito-infested room. The recipient family employing the service of the child-servant however does not give much thought to the fact that the child is now within a new culture, probably as an illegal immigrant and likely to be homesick and lonely. They pay little attention to the child-servant's unresolved immigration status and do little or nothing about it.

The child-servant, on the other hand, begins to realise he is on a distinctly different social stratum from his carers and is treated unequally in a society that promotes equality.

As the child gets older, he begins to become conscious of the reality of his situation, namely, that he is stuck in a rut. The child may soon realise that he has no identity in the United Kingdom, that he is being used and abused as a cheap domestic and has no future in the prevailing circumstances.

Sometimes exposure at school and within the United Kingdom environment also mean the child has changed; he is no longer the impoverished, wide-eyed innocent that came to the United Kingdom a few years earlier and has now been told and understands that children have rights which are enforceable in the United Kingdom. The child intends to fight for his own rights - and correctly so. He may then be fortunate to access appropriate services or speak to people who may be able to help him fight his cause and remedy the situation.

The scenarios described above may appear a somewhat rosy picture of the experience of some trafficked children, such as those going to school and just being made to do household chores. More worrying scenarios are when the child has been kept at home as a domestic and does not attend school, but one day he leaves the home and goes missing. It is very likely that the recipient family would not report him missing to the police if he was brought in on another person's passport for fear of being seen as harbouring a child in their home who has no identity and who does not exist in the system. Far more sinister is the possibility that the child could die or even be killed by a member of the recipient's family. As the child never existed within the system in the first place, such a child is unlikely to be missed. The evil repercussions of child-trafficking go far beyond the obvious.

'Adam', The Faceless Child: You may be aware of the tragic case of 'Adam', the African boy whose torso was found in the River Thames in September 2001 and which remained a twenty-first century mystery until he was identified as 6 year old Ikpomwosa in March 2011 after a ten-year police investigation. The conclusion of which was that he was killed and used for ritualistic purposes. Also significant is the fact that he was a trafficked child and there was no record of him in the United Kingdom system either with the health, education or immigration services.

There have also been reports of children kept indoors all day, working from dawn to dusk - cleaning and cooking, starved, beaten, used as sex slaves, raped and not given a chance of education. There have been other sinister reports of carers torturing child-servants by putting pepper in their eyes or their private parts; or as in the case of Ikpomwosa, being killed for ritualistic purposes.

This type of child abuse may apply to only a very tiny minority of Africans in the United Kingdom, we must however remember that *every child matters*, and one child experiencing the trauma of child-trafficking and its attendant abuses is a child too many. No child should be treated as having fewer rights simply because of the circumstances of his or her birth.

Domestic Servant Work: United Kingdom laws recognise that adults, not children, can work as domestic helpers and there are avenues to pursue this appropriately within the confines of the law.

Interestingly, a pensioner from Africa has also been convicted of trafficking and exploiting an adult servant. The pensioner's prosecution was based on the *ill-treatment* and *exploitation* of the woman she brought into the country legally as a servant. This pensioner fulfilled the legal aspect of bringing the woman into the United Kingdom lawfully, but failed to treat her appropriately within the employment law of the land.

It is imperative therefore that the domestic helper must be an adult in the first instance and must come in with the right visa under certain conditions. The employment arrangement or contract must be legal and fair within the confines of United Kingdom employment laws with consideration given for the minimum wage and fair employment conditions.

Bringing a child into the United Kingdom or accepting one for domestic servitude is not only morally wrong, but is also a heinous crime and must be stopped. Report your concerns about a trafficked child to the police or the children social services department in your area. Seek independent legal advice if you require further help in this area.

CASE 11 - CHILD DOMESTIC

Chuma and Chika married as young doctors in a West African country and immigrated to the United Kingdom shortly afterwards. They worked hard to pass their medical licensing examinations when they arrived and tried to start a family at the same time.

Fortunately, they both passed their examinations, and got good but very demanding jobs as medical doctors, often working shift patterns. Chika was pleased to fall pregnant shortly into the beginning of her career as a medical doctor and they were very happy when their son, 'Chuma Junior,' whom they both fondly called 'CJ', was born. Chika however suffered from sickle cell anaemia and the pregnancy, birth and early care of CJ took its toll on her health.

When CJ turned 2 years old, Chika began planning for a second child, as in her words, she wanted, "pregnancy years over and done with quickly." She did not appear to have fully considered how she would cope with being a wife and a mother, as well as carry on with her career and how she will deal with her health issues. Chuma constantly thought about this and it was his idea and suggestion that they bring over a housemaid, Grace, a 14 year old girl from their country to help out.

Grace had left her village approximately eight months earlier to live and work in the city as a housemaid with Chuma's mother. Grace was spoken highly of, although she spoke little English and had had only primary school education. She was an orphan who moved in with a maternal aunt after her mother died. The aunt found it difficult to care for her five children as well as four of her sister's. Grace was thus loaned out as a domestic servant to Chuma's mother in return for her basic needs being met and a small monthly payment to her aunt.

Chuma's mother arranged for Grace to be taken to the United Kingdom by a woman she was introduced to who charged a fee and made all the necessary arrangements. Grace was excited at the prospect of going to the United Kingdom and often day-dreamed about what it would be like when she got there. She was in awe as she travelled from the airport to her new home in the United Kingdom, marvelling at her new surroundings.

She cleaned the rooms, carried out general chores around the house, ironed, ran simple errands, and attended to CJ with whom she also shared a room with two single beds. She was polite, honest and obedient. Grace's basic needs were met and a private tutor came to the home once a week to help with her English and numeracy. A small sum of money was also sent to her aunt regularly via Chuma's mother.

She was allowed to watch television when she finished her chores, but she was often bored. She frequently thought of how she used to race the other domestic servants in the neighbourhood to the local taps to fetch water when she lived with Chuma's mother. They would then take turns to tell each other ridiculous fabricated short stories on their way back, shrieking with laughter. The highlight of Grace's week in the United Kingdom now was going to church with the family on Sundays - she loved to sing, dance, listen to the sermon and chat to the other girls. She always dressed nicely in the lovely clothes and shoes Chika bought her for outings. Grace began to wish she was one of the teenage girls in church who went to school and lived with their parents.

After about a year of living in the home, Grace began to build a small network of friends in the area and quickly picked up the basics of the English language from her friends, tutor and television. Initially, Chika and Chuma were pleased that Grace had made a few friends locally and that her English had improved greatly. They however became concerned when they noticed that Grace had begun to sneak out at night and appeared to bring strangers into the home whenever they went out. She gradually became rude and disobedient and various items began to go missing from the house. Grace started to answer Chika back and the confrontations about the missing items yielded no results.

Chika insisted on punishing Grace after she discovered that Grace now had a boyfriend (a young man had called at the house at a time when he did not expect Chika to be in).

There was a physical struggle between them as Grace tried to stop Chika seizing all Grace's nice clothing, shoes and accessories as punishment. Chika locked all the items up in her room and banned Grace from going out.

Grace left the house anyway and was missing for three days - it appeared she went to her boyfriend's house. Chika and Chuma did not report Grace missing to the police - simply waiting for her to return. On the fourth day, Chika was visited at home by the police after Grace had reported that she was routinely beaten, starved on occasions, had never been to school and was locked in the house over a two-year period.

The story sensationally made it to the pages of the local papers and Chuma and Chika were charged with cruelty, enslavement and false imprisonment although the case was eventually dropped. Chika who had only recently discovered she was pregnant again a few weeks before Grace went missing, lost the pregnancy, and the whole experience had an adverse effect on Chuma's career. Grace was placed at a foster carer's by the local authority. Her immigration status which remains unresolved, is currently being addressed by a solicitor.

CHAPTER 6

Private Fostering

Many adults care for other people's children, whether on a short or long term basis. If the arrangement is longer than a few days or weeks it could be deemed a private fostering arrangement (PFA).

Private fostering is a private arrangement made between a parent and another person who is not a close relative of the child to care for that child for a period of more than twenty-eight days continuously. A privately-fostered child is one under the age of 16 years old, or 18 years old if the child is disabled. It is not the same as children in the care of the local authority who are placed with foster carers. It is expected that the PFA will be initiated and funded in most cases by the parent.

Close relatives who a child can live with and who will not be classified as private foster carers (PFCs) by the fostering regulations include: brothers, sisters, aunts, uncles, grandparents or step-parents, by full or half-blood or marriage. Anyone else, no matter how close to the child or parent they may be, will be deemed a PFC; for example, a cousin of the child or the parents.

If a child is living with a close relative such as those mentioned above, it is not a PFA but kinship care, and there is no need for the local authority to be made aware, unless of course, the child or carer has a need that requires external support as may be the case where a person has a disability.

If however, the child is living with very close first or second cousins, it will still be considered a PFA.

According to the British Association of Adoption and Fostering (BAAF) there could be between 15,000 and 20,000 children in the United Kingdom who are currently being privately fostered. There are many circumstances that could make a birth parent feel unable to care for their child, and believe that it would be best for them to make an arrangement for the child to be cared for by someone else. This could arise for example, when a family is in crisis.

Common situations of private fostering occur after separation or divorce of the parents, during a difficult period in parenting a child (usually teenagers), after the death of the main caregiver, when parents study or have to take up employment away from home or when parents feel it is a better opportunity for the child's education and health needs to be met in the United Kingdom.

Africans and Private Fostering in the United Kingdom

Many African parents in the 1950s, 60s, and 70s privately fostered their children to white families whilst studying in the United Kingdom and the practice still exists to date.

There are currently many African children who have been sent to the United Kingdom to study and be cared for by relatives and others whilst their birth parents remain overseas. Although, this is an acceptable form of childcare in the United Kingdom and is covered by legislation and guidance, many children in PFAs are considered to be vulnerable, as they now live with a carer who is not a close relative and who has no parental responsibility for them.

The law tries to ameliorate this vulnerability, and perhaps the most significant part of the law in this area is the requirement that the local authority in which the child now resides needs to be informed that such an arrangement is about to take place or has

> *...many children in PFAs are considered to be vulnerable, as they now live with a carer who is not a close relative and who has no parental responsibility for them.*

taken place. This is to ensure that children in those circumstances are being properly safeguarded and monitored by trained professionals and any outstanding needs they may have are being addressed and met.

What is known as kinship care or PFA in the United Kingdom is common practice in African communities and remains an informal family and community arrangement ungoverned by the state. In many parts of Africa, there is sometimes little distinction between a close blood or biological relation and one who is not. What counts is the relationship that has been developed over the years. This lack of distinction is perhaps what led to the tradition of calling adult family and non-family members aunties and uncles in some African countries and can often be confusing to those less familiar with this practice.

Many Africans grew up with many aunties, uncles and cousins who are not blood relatives but have been informally adopted as part of the family. Several have imported this practice to the United Kingdom, sending children over to various types of uncles and aunties for a better life.

As Lord Laming commented in his report on Victoria Climbie,

> Entrusting children to relatives in Europe who can
> offer opportunities that would not be available
> to them in the Ivory Coast was not uncommon in
> Victoria's parents' society.

PFAs are seriously under-reported to local authorities as required by law, as many people consider it a private issue. Many Africans may struggle in particular with the description of who is considered a close relative under United Kingdom law and informing a public body of childcare arrangements that are deemed a private family matter.

Strange as the concept of private fostering and the required notifications may seem, many will agree that it is a good idea, especially in a society with little informal support systems to ensure that children are safe, their new carers and absent parents are supported and a safety buffer is created for all concerned. It is important to consider factors such as those below before initiating a PFA as a parent or agreeing to become a PFC.

Significant Factors in Private Fostering Arrangements

The Child's Status: A trafficked African child bears similarity to a private fostered child in many ways. A clear distinction will be the child's status in the United Kingdom.

If the child's parents live in Africa and the proper channels were used to obtain a visa for the purpose of him coming to live and study in the United Kingdom, there is likely to be a presumption that it is a PFA. If checks are conducted by the local authority and the child's passport is missing or irregular and there is no clarity on how the child came to live in the United Kingdom, there is likely to be suspicion that the child is trafficked, even if he attends school.

This may however not be the case, but could put the carer at risk of being labelled a child trafficker especially if the relationship between child and carer is poor, or if other aspects of the child's needs are not adequately met. Also, having a child in your care with no clear immigration status could make it difficult for that child to register with the surgery, education providers, maintain contact with his birth family or return to his birth family at the end of the PFA.

The Child's Relationship: Some Africans may find the definition of close relative under United Kingdom private fostering regulations strange or even offensive. One can understand this, as many Africans are closer to several non-blood aunties and uncles than they are to their blood relatives.

However, the regulations are based on research findings that children who do not live with their birth parents or close relatives are more vulnerable and more likely to be abused, as it is easier to feel a sense of obligation, affection and care for a child who is your blood relative than one who is not. You are more likely to have a stronger attachment to a child you are closely related to and you are more likely to put yourself out more for that child than one to whom you are not related. Remember the popular phrase, 'blood is thicker than water'? That adage proves true in those findings.

This is especially so in the United Kingdom where there is no wide network of support to help you raise the child. A child who is a close relative is also more likely to be better grafted into your household, as he is likely to see himself as part of your family, as opposed to one with whom you do not have a blood relationship. If the child is a close relative as defined by the regulations, the authorities will assume he is part of your family and this will not be considered a PFA which has to be reported.

The Paramountcy Principle: This principle suggests that the child's need will take first priority and be paramount in all matters relating to him, but we know that this is not always the case.

Whose need is being considered first in initiating a PFA? In many situations, it is likely to be that of the parents. It therefore suggests that a PFA may not have prioritised or considered the child's needs and wishes, as it is unlikely that many children would choose to live with a stranger and apart from their parents - unless they are experiencing significant difficulties with them.

While parents' circumstances may make it impractical for their children to live with them for a period of time, it is wise to bear in mind not only the children's ages and their wishes, but also to ensure as much as possible that they understand the situation, agree with the changes and are happy with the arrangement. Consideration also needs to be given to how other aspects of the child's needs (religious and cultural) will be met; for example, where an African child is cared for by white PFCs.

Financial Needs: Children have needs that have financial implications on whoever is responsible for them. It does not take a soothsayer to predict that there are on-going monetary consequences in caring for a child in the United Kingdom. Most parents have made allowances in their wages for their children's needs and sometimes have to make huge sacrifices.

At times there is no clarity on whom the responsibility of meeting some of the financial needs of the privately-fostered child falls. In the case of Victoria Climbie, there was an assumption that the great-aunt would meet all her essential needs. If it is agreed that the birth parents will have responsibility for the child's financial needs, a reasonable amount as well as the frequency and the means by which the money will be sent all need to be agreed from the onset. Provision should also be made and contingency plans put in place for emergency funds to be readily available should monies not be sent on time or at all. The PFC also needs to be aware of any State benefits she may be entitled to in caring for the child.

Space and Time: The PFC will also need to consider how much physical space or room they have and can afford to give to a child in their care. They will need to consider if they have the emotional energy to care for another person's child without being neglectful or abusive in other ways. There will also be time implications such as attending educational and leisure activities with the child and on behalf of the birth parents as they would their own.

Effect on the PFC's Family: A lot of PFCs do not think of the long-term implications of caring for someone else's child, and agreements are reached on the spur of the moment without things being clearly thought through.

There are known cases where a child has come on holidays to the United Kingdom and the auntie who is sometimes just a close family friend, offers for the child to live with her family and to register him at a local school. The long-term implications for the PFC's spouse and children are not considered and many foster carers have taken on such a huge responsibility without consulting with other members of their household.

Even if the adult female carer in the home can make the child feel welcome, she would need to consider if her spouse and children would do the same. Family members may be unhappy or become fed up with sharing their space with someone who is neither a sibling nor close relative. The physical, emotional and psychological aspects of the arrangement on the child and the PFC's family need to be carefully considered.

Maintaining Contact: Like most people who are separated from family members, privately-fostered children are likely to miss their birth families and feel homesick. There will therefore be the need for regular contact. It is important that birth parents and the rest of the family maintain contact with the child as often as possible or as needed.

The parent and PFC need to agree on when, where, with whom, how and how often contact will be made. While it is best for these sorts of arrangements to be flexible, some PFCs have found it difficult to accommodate parents who visit on an ad hoc basis, and some parents may feel resentful that they cannot see their child when they want to do so. The child may also want to see the parents and siblings more frequently or less so. Telephone, internet and mail contact should also be encouraged where possible.

Period of Arrangement: There needs to be clarity on how long the private fostering arrangement will last for and all parties especially the child, need to know this. Birth parents have been known to mislead children on how long they will be living away for. There are also several cases both past and present where PFCs had developed strong attachments to the child in their care - some of the children having been with them since infancy - and refused to hand the child back to the parents.

They fought the parents in court as they felt the parents were not able to care for the child properly or did not deserve the child who had spent most of his or her lifetime with them, and in their view had a stronger bond to them than his parents. Each case will of course be decided on its own merits, with the court ruling in favour of the PFCs where it is considered to be in the child's best interests.

Contingency Plans: Consideration also needs to be given to the possibility of the placement failing before the end of the period initially agreed. Examples are when the PFC falls ill, moves out of the area or country or has new responsibilities which make carrying on the role difficult.

It is not uncommon to find children in PFAs with no contingency plans, or who have simply been passed from one PFC to another on an ad hoc basis - once the last one has become fed up. There have also been arrangements where the child has been abandoned by the birth parents who simply vanished without a trace. Needless to say, this sort of instability is a form of abuse in itself.

Parenting Styles: Parents and PFCs who have got on well prior to the PFA have been known to fall out over the parenting of the child.

The PFC who is expected to take on the role of a parent for the child may have a different child-rearing style from the birth parent. It only stands to reason that the PFC will apply what they believe to be appropriate child-rearing techniques. The birth parent may be an authoritative parent, while the PFC may be more permissive or vice-versa.

For example, one may believe a child should receive regular pocket money for leisure activities, go out with his peers regularly, and not do household chores, while the other may believe otherwise. The child may also be confused and find it difficult to adjust to a new style of parenting. What happens when the birth parent is unhappy about or disagrees with how the child is being parented?

The above are a few important areas that need to be considered and explored by both birth parents and PFCs before a PFA is proposed or agreed to. The role of the local authority is to support the process and ensure it is a positive and appropriate care-giving experience, especially for the child.

Victoria Climbie: The Private-Fostered Child

Victoria Climbie was actually a privately-fostered child according to the laws in the United Kingdom. She was a 7 year old girl who left the Ivory Coast in November 1998 initially to live with her great-aunt in France before coming with her to London in April 1999. Her parents had verbally agreed to her great-aunt taking her abroad to live and school for a better life. As it was a great-aunt, it was a private fostering arrangement (PFA).

Thinking she was the child of her great-aunt, Victoria Climbie was not recognised as a child in a private fostering arrangement by the authorities in the United Kingdom and her needs, as such a child, were not assessed. She eventually became a severely abused child and ultimately died from the extreme physical abuse she suffered at the hands of her great-aunt and her boyfriend in February 2000.

Tragically, instead of the presence of another adult making it easier to care for Victoria, the abuse seemed to escalate when the aunt met her new boyfriend. Her great-aunt's circumstance had changed and she probably no longer needed Victoria's company who increasingly appeared to have become an unwanted nuisance to both her great-aunt and the boyfriend. Victoria's birth parents never saw her again after she left the Ivory Coast in 1998 and were not in frequent telephone contact with her.

Her great-aunt may have had some good intentions at the time she removed Victoria from her parents in Ivory Coast. The great-aunt had perhaps made an emotional decision at the time she took Victoria away from her home and never considered the extent of the needs of a 7 year old child in the United Kingdom without the customary African family support. It is possible that it became increasingly difficult for her to care for Victoria and the abuse gradually escalated.

In many African societies, children are still the collective responsibility of the family and the community in which they belong. As is popularly said in Africa, 'it takes a village to raise a child.' It may therefore be easier in those societies to raise children without giving much consideration to the extent of the relationship between the carer and the child.

The United Kingdom is more of an individualist society with the nuclear family bearing most of the weight and responsibility of parenting without the extended family and community involvement. Also the needs of children in the United Kingdom are different culturally and this could further place a higher demand on the parenting role without the corresponding informal support that could perhaps make things easier. All these are factors to be carefully considered in fostering out your child or agreeing to be a PFC.

It is important to note that the local authority in which a child lives has a role in ensuring the needs of every privately-fostered child are appropriately met, and it is against the law not to report a private fostering arrangement. A social worker ought to visit on a regular basis to offer advice, support and ensure that the arrangement is still suitable for all concerned, considering all the factors highlighted above and more.

If you know of a child being privately fostered please do not ignore it. Explain to the parents or carer the need to notify the local authority's private fostering team or do so yourself.

CHAPTER 7

Special Children, Special Needs

Every parent hopes for a healthy and able-bodied child after a nine-month pregnancy. Finding out your child has a disability can therefore be bewildering and difficult for most parents. It is normal for parents to experience a whole range of mixed feelings which some never recover from. If the child is severely disabled, it is the loss felt, at the denial of seeing that child develop into an independent adult, who will perhaps get married one day, have a career and children of their own. A lot depends on the type and extent of the disability, the attitude and perception of the parents, their socio-economic status and the community to which the family belongs.

According to 'Contact a Family', there are 770,000 disabled children under the age of 16 in the United Kingdom. That equates to approximately one child in twenty. Some disabled children are more vulnerable to abuse and it is not difficult to understand why.

Some children with disabilities are highly dependent and demanding of their parents' time and attention, which can leave parents constantly exhausted from the physical demands of parenting. Also unlike normal children, the demands do not necessarily decrease with age and growth and the parents cannot inevitably look forward to a day when the child will be independent.

This lifelong dependency can create stress for the parents and further vulnerability to the child where there is an acute lack of support. Parental stress and lack of support are major risk factors in all aspects of child abuse, thus placing disabled children at a higher level of risk than others. Despite the daily challenges, financial constraints and lack of support, many parents continue to give their time willingly as carers to their disabled children who to them and others remain very special and loved.

In many countries and cultures including parts of Africa, the presence of a disability, especially a severe one in a child at birth can be a huge social stigma. Some cultures blame one of the parents, usually the mother, believing without evidence, that the cause of the disability is perhaps genetically linked to her and therefore her fault. In fact, disabilities are seen by some as punishment for sins committed or a curse placed on an individual.

Many Africans continue to believe that the root cause of several disabilities lies in the spirit world and this belief in itself can affect how the child's needs are being addressed. There are also unspoken assumptions in many cultures that disabled children are less important than other children, or that neglecting them does not matter much as they are not seen as having the same cognitive abilities as other children. Opportunities are also limited for this group of children and their parents in numerous developing countries where many remain hidden and unwanted.

Generally, even within the majority white population in the United Kingdom, disabled children are known to have fewer outside contacts and have a reduced capacity to resist or avoid abuse due to communication or mobility difficulties. Some disabled children may be unable or unwilling to complain and are more vulnerable to intimidation and exploitation. In the United Kingdom, disabled children are over-represented in the population of children looked after by local authorities and are more likely to be placed in residential settings away from their homes due to the heavy demands and stress on their family.

Many African parents of disabled children in the United Kingdom face extra challenges due to limited socio-economic and environmental resources. As immigrants, the informal extended family system which could have constituted a network of support for them is also unlikely to exist in the United Kingdom.

A study undertaken by the Joseph Rowntree Foundation showed that families from ethnic minority groups (including Africans) are at a greater disadvantage than their white counterparts in meeting their disabled children's needs. Many were less likely to claim or be awarded benefits at the higher rate of the disability living allowance or invalid care allowance. Professor Ahmad, co-author of the report, concluded that this disadvantage meant many of these families were 'living on the edge'.

Some African parents may believe that their disabled child is their lot and they should bear full responsibility for the child. This may prevent them from seeking help even when they are clearly struggling. This could however put the child at a further disadvantage preventing aspects of his needs being addressed and met. It could also lead to poorer psychological and physical wellbeing of the parents.

The Grief Process

Grief is a deeply painful, albeit normal human reaction to loss. The death of someone close is probably what comes to mind when thinking of grief and loss. Loss can however occur in several ways with the grief being more intense the more significant the loss is. Many parents of children with disabilities go through a grief process in dealing with the significant loss of not having a normal child. Many are likely to experience the DABDA grief process as defined by Elisabeth Kübler-Ross. DABDA refers to: **D**enial **A**nger **B**argaining **D**epression **A**cceptance.

The experience of each stage does not necessarily follow sequentially as stated above, and may fluctuate. Parents who experience their child's disability as a loss of a normal child and family life are however likely to go through each stage.

The loss usually starts with ***Denial*** - which is the stage of not accepting that the disability exists in the child. It may take a while to absorb the shock and the parent may pretend the child does not have the disability or that the disability will go away or not have much of an impact on the child or the family.

Denial is usually temporary and this gives way to the next stage, which is ***Anger***. Parents are likely to become angry and express this anger at themselves, their spouse, the child and those around them. It is at this stage that they may be thinking and wondering, 'Why me? How could this be happening to us?' or 'This is so unfair.'

Bargaining is the third stage in the grief process and this involves hoping the situation will change, albeit slightly. This bargaining is usually done with a higher power with promises of change for a less difficult diagnosis. For example, a parent of a child who is unable to talk or walk as part of the disability, may try bargaining that the child be just able to talk and they will be satisfied despite the manifestation of the other signs of disability in the child. When this does not work in reality they are likely to move to the fourth stage, which is depression.

Depression is where parents begin to understand the disability and the extent of the challenges they are faced with. This in turn leads to low moments and it is common for parents to feel sad, uncertain about the current situation, possibly regretting having the child and fearing what the future holds.

Acceptance is the stage where parents begin to move past the depression and come to terms with the disability of their child. They may begin to see it as a situation in their lives to manage and cope with, expressing thoughts and words such as, 'We can handle this'; 'It is going to be okay'; 'We can't change the past'; 'We will be fine'. At this stage, parents find new strength which enables them to begin to move on purposefully in spite of the disability.

Impact of Grief: The grief process is known to have a huge impact on parents and their relationship with each other and their other children. Many parents have also reported lack of sleep, tiredness, financial difficulties and problems at work since having a child with a disability. These pressures are likely to be contributory factors in the higher rate of separation and divorce amongst parents of disabled children. Several parents have however sought support through relationship counselling which many have found helpful. Many parents have also reported that being able to communicate openly with their partner and having time away together from the child has helped their relationship and the grief process.

Child in Need

Section 17 of The Children Act 1989 recognises a child with disabilities as *a child in need*. This means the local authority where the child lives has a duty to safeguard and promote the child's welfare and provide a range of services to meet his or her needs. Most local authorities in England and Wales have a Children with Disabilities Team that begins the process of engagement with the child and his family with an assessment of the child's needs. It is important as the parent of a child with disabilities, that you refer your child for an assessment as early as possible.

Parents must remember that they are best placed to be an advocate for their child's needs. It is therefore important that they are as clear and detailed as they can be during assessments. Language should not be a barrier since local authorities provide interpreter services to parents whose first language is not English as part of the assessment process.

Some day-care, respite care or short-breaks may be necessary to enhance the child's development as well as to give the parents a break on a regular basis depending on the level of the child's needs. The level of support each local authority provides depends largely on the extent of the disability and needs of the child and family as well as the local authority's resources and the demand on it. The support could include direct financial payments to parents to buy their own support needs. It could also include linking parent and child with community resources that can support the role of the parent-carer of a disabled child as well as support the disabled child's needs as an individual.

Information about local voluntary support groups is one of the most valuable resources you can get from your local authority, especially if your child's disability and associated needs are assessed to be on a lower level and more intense support or funds cannot be provided.

Statement of Special Educational Needs (SEN)

A child with learning disabilities may need a statement of Special Education Needs (SEN). This is a formal document detailing a child's learning difficulties and the help that will be given. If your child needs help at school beyond what the teachers can provide, a statement of SEN will ensure he receives the right help with his or her education. The statement is usually only necessary if the school is unable to meet a child's needs on its own and requires extra resources. Statements differ and will usually include the difficulties as they relate to a particular child.

Difficulties which a statement can help to address include: physical and sensory disabilities, maintaining concentration, regulating emotions and behaviour, as well as learning to read or to write. Some parents may be anxious and unclear as to how a statement may affect their child and due to fear of stigma or shame, may decide to minimise the child's difficulties, refuse or delay assessment.

The local authority however has a legally binding duty to ensure the support outlined in the statement is provided. All support identified in the statement will be tailored to the specific needs of the child. The statement should be a positive step for a child and should be an evolving live document amended as necessary to recognise changes in the child's circumstances and needs.

As a parent, the statement can provide you with insight into the area of schooling that your child finds particularly challenging as well as things that can be done to make home or school life more manageable for the child. Parent partnership services are available in most local authorities and are designed specifically to offer advice, support and information on disabilities and statements of special education needs to parents. The contact details of your local parent partnership service can be obtained from your local authority office, library or the internet.

Present and Future

More and more children and adults with disabilities are living longer, fuller, more enriched lives now than they used to do many years ago. With the right care and support many have been able to express skills, gifts and talents that people never thought they could. Many disabled children also continue to be a great source of joy to members of their family and community. Many disabled children also have fulfilling and loving relationships with their parents and other family members.

It is therefore important to educate those around you, especially those within your family, community and network of support on the disability and needs of your child. You must develop a positive attitude as much as possible in advocating, caring for and meeting your child's needs and this is likely to encourage those around you to do the same.

Parents must however maintain a careful balance and ensure they take care of themselves and their other relationships. Relationships with spouses and other children are especially important as this will have an impact on the child with disabilities. Spouses and siblings can feel left out or neglected if the disabled child is always the main focus and priority for one parent.

A major worry for the parents of disabled children is the future; particularly the future of their disabled child when they, the parents are no longer around. It is important for a parent to know that they are not alone and many other parents have successfully passed through the stage they are at currently.

There are many national and local support groups in the United Kingdom which cater for people with disabilities from childhood to adulthood as well as for their families. These groups can help with each family's situation. It is also important that parents seek help at the early stages of knowing their child has a disability, as early intervention has been known to improve many situations, for example in managing expected future symptoms and early modification of the child's behaviour.

Early intervention could help prevent a breakdown in the family relationship and in the child being placed away from home. The contact details of Advisory Centre for Education (ACE) and Contact a Family (CAF) which provides information, advice, support and resources for families on all disabilities is provided in the resource section at the end of this book.

CASE 12 - DOWN'S SYNDROME

Elsie tells us about parenting a child with Down's Syndrome:

"I had broken off the relationship with Seun's father while I was still pregnant with him. I was already in my forties; I had a good job, had my own home and was willing to carry on my life as a single parent.

It was a relatively easy birth and my friend, Rachel, stayed with me during labour. The doctor told me Seun had Down's syndrome. I could also tell from looking at him. I broke down and cried. I didn't want to hold him and handed him to Rachel who tried hard to comfort me.

I took him home a few days later, despondent and ashamed. I wanted to kill both of us. I rarely went out with him, leaving him at home with my mother who came from Africa to help me care for him. When I took him out, I pulled the pushchair cover over him as far as possible so no one could really see him. When people looked at him, I could feel the look of pity they gave me. I became very depressed and would have probably killed both of us if my mother had not been around. That was fifteen years ago.

I love Seun and he is the most important person in my life. He is such a lovely child, so full of fun and laughter and truly enjoys life. He can't read or write properly, but can make himself simple meals and swims like a fish! He is learning to manage his personal care well and is so sensitive and warm.

It is almost like he knows the world needs more love and is always smiling, always kind to people and willing to help, without realising that he's intruding a lot of the time! He knows when I am feeling low and would come over, put his arms around me, tell me he loves me and that everything will be alright.

My local support group has also helped tremendously. I especially love the short breaks and days out with other parents. It's nice to be with people who really know what it feels like to be the parent of a child with special needs."

CASE 13 - AUTISM

Amma and Kofi are immigrants who came to the United Kingdom in the 1990s. Now both in their forties and well-established in their careers, they were overjoyed when Amma fell pregnant again five years after their first child, Joy, was born. They had been desperate for another child before now and this time it was confirmed to be a boy who they would call David.

The first year and a half after David's birth was sheer bliss emotionally, the family felt complete and fulfilled as a unit. Amma had however began to notice since David was about a year old, that he was not maintaining appropriate eye contact, or smiling back at her as his sister Joy did when she was about the same age. The couple waited a while and it was shortly after David's second birthday that they received the devastating news that David was autistic.

Amma and Kofi both went through personal periods of deep grief. Eventually, with Kofi's support, Amma took on the main caring and advocacy role for David. She sought information via the local authority and the internet on autism and on how best to care for David.

The couple fluctuated between the various stages of grief sometimes feeling hopeful and accepting their situation while at other times feeling guilty, utterly depressed and despondent. They prayed together as a family and continued to attend their friendly and supportive family church over a period of three years.

However, Amma was deeply hurt when she began to notice that church members treated the now 5 year old David as if he did not exist. Some of the adults avoided him completely and never invited him to participate in the children's church activities or to any of their children's birthday parties. Amma addressed the situation with the leader of the children's church who apologised for not including David in the children's activities. The leader explained that as she was not familiar with

David's disability, she did not know how to help him or involve him with the other children.

It was only then, that Amma realised that people simply did not know how to respond to David. It was easier for them to ignore him and treat him as invisible outside of his special needs school setting where the staff were trained and experienced. Amma became more proactive in being David's advocate and discussed with the leader on how best to include David in activities with the other children. The leader also agreed for Amma to come into the class to explain autism and David's needs to the other children. Being children, many of them asked the simple but pertinent questions. "Why does he scream loudly?" "How do we know what he wants?" "Will he hit us if we play with him?" Amma was able to address these in a way that helped the other children better understand David's needs as well as develop empathy for his disability.

Amma and Kofi still experience some occasional low moments about what the future holds for David, but they both clearly love him and have also made significant adjustments. Their social worker has been particularly supportive in helping them access local groups and accompanied Amma and David on their first visit to the toy library. Kofi has also begun to take David for swimming lessons which they both enjoy and this gives Amma some time alone with Joy. As Kofi philosophically put it to Amma on occasions, "We don't get to choose our children, they are simply gifts from God to do our best with" and "God must consider us special to give us a child with special needs to raise for Him."

David is now accepted and included in the children's church group activities with one-to-one support from volunteers. When no volunteer is available to support him, one of his parents volunteers for the session. Many of the children also like to help out and take turns in supporting David. He is now much better understood and seen as a valued part of the children's church group which he thoroughly enjoys and continues to attend a special needs school.

Amma and Kofi are taking a week's holiday away together as a couple for the first time since David was born. David will be going on respite care for the week with carers who are gradually becoming familiar faces to him, while Joy will spend the time with aunty Brenda and uncle Wajde, close friends of Amma and Kofi, who have two daughters of their own.

CHAPTER 8

Your Child's Education

Education is compulsory for all children between the ages of 5 to 16 in the United Kingdom. The age of compulsory education has been increased by the Education and Skills Act 2008 to 17 years old from 2013 and 18 years old from 2015 when students will have the option of either staying on in school or enrolling on some other training programme.

There is currently a national curriculum which all state schools are required to follow until children are 16 years old. The education system in the United Kingdom has changed in many ways over the years and continues to do so. There is a lot for parents to understand and various parts can appear complex even for parents who have always lived in the United Kingdom.

Stages of State Education

Entry into Schools: The process of entry into state nursery, primary and secondary schools is not automatic and you need to apply for your child if you want a place for him in a state school. The local authority the child lives in coordinates applications and admissions and is under obligation to offer all children that apply within its area a school place.

You and your child can make three choices of state schools within your area, but as each school has its own admissions criteria you may not necessarily get a place in any of your choices. It is always wise to find out the admissions criteria for the schools you chose and how closely you meet them. For example, some criteria are based on how close you live to the school, if other siblings of your child attend the school already or your child has a special need that makes it the most accessible school.

Detailed information about pre-schools, primary and secondary schools, post-16 education and universities as well as their admissions criteria can be found via websites such as www.gov.co.uk.

Pre-School: Many parents start by using child-minders, au pairs, nannies, grandparents and private nurseries to care for their children when they return to work after their child's birth or maternity/paternity leave. Many private nurseries and child-minders accept children from about 3 months to 5 years old. Some of these nurseries are simply care alternatives with little structure around educating the child and you may want to clarify how the setting will meet the needs of your older pre-school child as you gauge the level of his maturity. Remember though, that many of these settings do very well in developing children's social skills and confidence. Many other nurseries begin a pre-school curriculum when the children are between 2 and 4 years old.

All 3 and 4 year olds in England and Wales are currently entitled to fifteen hours of free nursery education for 38 weeks of the year. Many working parents needing more childcare provision claim for the cost of looking after their children outside of the fifteen hours by applying for Child Tax Credit or Working Tax Credit. Some of these benefits are for those on a lower income, are means-tested and dependent on your immigration status.

There is a range of pre-school settings that provide the free fifteen hours education including playgroups, nursery schools and children's centres. Every local authority has a list of these pre-school providers which can be obtained from their family information service.

Primary School: There are four key stages in the national curriculum. State primary schools adhere to the first two stages for children aged 5 to 11 years (Reception Class to Year 6). Many subjects are compulsory as part of the national curriculum at these stages including Mathematics, English and Science.

Children in Years 1 and 2 are usually in the first stage known as Key Stage 1, while those in Years 3 to 6 are on different levels in Key Stage 2. The levels in the Key Stages are used to measure your child's progress in comparison to other children. Most children will be on Level 2 at the end of Key Stage 1 (Year 2) and Level 4 at the end of Key Stage 2 (Year 6).

Primary school is the time when parents can probably best help their children with their literacy and numeracy skills. Ensuring their homework is well completed is a very important part that parents can play in supporting their child's learning. Parents can also ask the child's teachers, who are likely to be in the best position to do so, to recommend specific learning materials to support the child's learning at home. There are also many free online tools that can be used or downloaded free.

Standard Assessment Tests (SATS): SATS is an acronym for Standard Assessment Tests which are given to measure children's progress at different stages in primary and secondary school. They are mandatory for all state primary schools with the first one taken at the end of Year 2, the second at the end of Year 6 and the last one in Year 9 in secondary school. In Year 2, your child's ability will be assessed by his teacher using samples of his work in Reading, Writing, Mathematics, Science, Spellings and Handwriting.

Most children are expected to achieve Level 2 at the end of Year 2. Each level is further distinguished by an 'a', 'b' or 'c' grade. For example, a grade of Level 2a shows a higher level of achievement than level 2c. The SATS in Year 6 are more formal, with children expected to prepare more intensely in English, Mathematics and Science.

The papers are marked externally and most children will be expected to achieve Level 4 at this stage with more academic children achieving Level 5. Below are the average levels for children according to the SATS Guide website - www.satsguide.co.uk.

Level W - Working towards Level 1, very weak

Level 1 - Average for a typical 5 year old

Level 2 - Average for a typical 7 year old

Level 3 - Average for a typical 9 year old

Level 4 - Average for a typical 11 year old

Level 5 - Average for a typical 13 year old

Level 6 - Average for a typical 14 year old

Level 7 - Above-average for a typical 14 year old

Level 8 - Only available in Mathematics

The website is a great resource for parents and children on SATS.

11-Plus Examinations: This is a selective examination taken in Year 6 by some students. It is usually held at the earlier part of the school year between October and February. The examinations are set as a way of determining which children are academically able to gain places in the remaining grammar schools in England which are in high demand. There is some confusion about the difference between this and the Key Stage 2 SATS.

SATS is a nationally approved examination and the Key Stage 2 tests are mandatory for all state primary schools and usually taken towards the end of Year 6 in May.

11-plus examinations on the other hand are voluntary examinations to gain entry into selective schools such as grammar schools. Bear in mind that the 11-plus examinations which are held earlier in Year 6 are set at a much higher level (Levels 5 and 6) than the Key Stage 2 SATS (Level 4) which is held towards the end of the school year.

In most cases, state schools and their curriculum prepare children only for the Key Stage 2 SATS, so parents who want their children to attend grammar schools would need to start preparing them early enough to attain a much higher level. Many parents start as early as Year 4 using various teaching aids or tutors. The 11-plus exams usually comprise English, Mathematics, Verbal and Non-verbal reasoning papers, whilst the SATS are Mathematics, English and science.

Some grammar schools and other independent schools may have different exams, so it is always best to check with the ones you want your child to attend. There is a list of grammar schools and more support in regard to the 11-plus exams on the website www.the11pluswebsite.co.uk.

Secondary School: State secondary schools are for pupils from Year 7 to 11 (for ages 11 to 16 years) with the majority of them in England and Wales being comprehensive schools that do not select entrants solely on a child's academic ability and some grammar schools which are selective. A child's level at the end of Year 9 (Key Stage 3) is usually determined by the teacher's assessment of his progress as there are no national tests.

It is important for parents to remain involved in their children's education at this stage. Make a habit of checking their school diaries and speak to their class teachers from time to time about their progress if possible. Children in Year 9 (Key Stage 3) choose a few out of a range of subjects they will study in Years 10 and 11 (Key Stage 4) with some subjects remaining compulsory such as: one modern foreign language (usually German, French or Spanish), English, Mathematics, Science, Physical Education, Citizenship and Information and Communication Technology (ICT). Their studies and examinations in many of these subjects eventually lead to GCSEs, BTECs and other nationally recognised qualifications at the end of Year 11.

After Year 11: Many children carry on schooling beyond the age of compulsory education at 16 years old or school Year 11 to the sixth forms in Years 12 and 13 which leads to qualifications in AS (Advanced Subsidiary) and A (Advanced) Levels. A-Levels are made up of the AS Level and the A2. Each part makes up 50% of the overall A-Level grade. A child can study the AS Level as a qualification on its own, or it can be the first half of the full A-Level. Depending on the school or college, a child can take the AS Level as the final qualification, or continue to the second year and go for the full A-Level. In the second year of a full A-Level, the student takes the A2 - this is not a separate qualification, but the second half of the A-Level. The A2 is designed to deepen the knowledge gained during the AS Level.

Other qualifications that can be obtained if they choose to stay on in education or training include the International Baccalaureate, National Vocational Qualifications (NVQs), diplomas and apprenticeships.

Many grammar schools opted for the International Baccalaureate (IB) instead of the AS and A Levels programme. The IB is also a two-year academically challenging programme. The IB is a well-recognised Diploma by many universities and accepted as an alternative to AS and A Levels.

National Vocational Qualifications (NVQs) on the other hand are work-based awards achieved through training and assessments. There are five levels in the NVQ and students must show that they have developed the competence to carry out their work to the required standard. Although traditionally known as vocational non-academic qualifications, NVQs are now being accepted in many universities depending on the course of study. Apprenticeships are also vocational forms of study where students work and earn some money, receive training and acquire qualifications as they develop their skills.

Other Educational Settings

After School Clubs: Many schools and voluntary organisations operate outside school hours to provide extra-curricular activities and various opportunities for children to develop their skills in areas other than the purely academic. Apart from extra-curricular activities being an opportunity to have

> *Activities and structured clubs can also keep your child safer, occupied and focused on what he enjoys thereby preventing idleness and boredom.*

some fun, exercise and develop a social network outside the school setting, many hidden talents have been discovered as children have taken part in areas such as various kinds of sports and music. Your child may discover his talent in an area early and go on to become a professional musician, athlete, footballer or swimmer.

Activities and structured clubs can also keep your child safer, occupied and focused on what he enjoys thereby preventing idleness and boredom. It is also worth bearing in mind that many bursaries and scholarships in private/ independent schools are also reserved for children with talents in other areas such as sports and music. Universities also use extra-curricular activities to differentiate between students of equal academic ability and your child will have to demonstrate his involvement and skills in other areas apart from the purely academic when he is completing his UCAS application forms.

Independent Schools: About 8% of school-aged children in the United Kingdom attend independent or private schools. Unlike state schools, these are not dependent on government taxes for funding, but are usually self-governed and financed through the payment of tuition fees and other investments. It is always wise to consider what the full cost of giving your child a private education will be, as there may be many other costs and charges that may not be included in what may be already high fees.

Some independent schools give means-tested bursaries and scholarships to students gifted in particular fields such as sports, music and the arts. Many of the schools have some form of selection with some, but not all based on academic abilities.

Some of the advantages of independent schools over state schools include parents being able to choose a school they feel is right for their child provided they can pay for it. The staff-to-pupil ratio is usually smaller than in state schools which mean a child is likely to receive more individual attention. Many of the schools are also of higher standards with students achieving good grades on average. Each school has its own admissions criteria and it is best to contact the schools directly or websites with information on a wide range of schools such as www.isc.co.uk and www.indschools.co.uk.

Faith Schools: These are schools that give preference to applicants who are of the faith of the school. Those that are state schools are however under obligation to take on children from other faiths if they are unable to fill up their school places. Many of the faith schools in the United Kingdom are classified as state schools with the governance of the school remaining with the faith group and funding coming from the state.

Faith State schools are still required to follow the national curriculum apart from religious studies which they can limit to their own beliefs. Faith schools have been expanded to include Muslim as well as Christian and Jewish schools. Some faith schools are also independent schools.

Boarding Schools: Boarding schools in the United Kingdom comprise of both state and independent schools. Independent boarding schools charge for both tuition fees and boarding facilities, while the state boarding schools only charge for boarding facilities. Admission to state boarding schools is limited to children who have right of residence in the United Kingdom.

On average, boarding schools can be less distracting and children may generally be safer than those who travel on a daily basis to day schools. It can help provide stability, structure and boundaries for a child whose parents travel regularly. It could also foster more independence in children than if they lived at home, preparing them better for adult life.

Boarding schools can however deny you of quality family time together. This could in turn have a negative effect on your relationship with your child as well as their sibling relationships when they are separated for long periods of time at an early age. Parents also miss opportunities to watch their children grow in various areas and may not get to exercise their parenting skills as much as they would have when they see their children daily. See the website for the State Boarding School Association www.sbsa.org.uk for information and guidance on state boarding schools.

Home Schooling: Parents have a right to educate their children at home in the United Kingdom and they do not have to follow the national curriculum or educate the child within formal school hours. The law however requires that children are educated to an appropriate standard for their age and ability. There is no state funding for home schooling and a local authority officer can visit to ensure the child is being educated to a satisfactory standard. More information about home schooling can be obtained from your local authority or from the government website www.gov.uk.

Universities: The University and College Admissions Service (UCAS) is the organisation responsible for managing entry into universities and other higher education institutions in the United Kingdom. There is a wide range of courses to study in various universities across the United Kingdom and there are many advantages to a higher education such as a university degree. It can increase your child's confidence and independence, increase financial prospects, open your child to various career options within and outside the United Kingdom and provide an opportunity to socialise with many more likeminded people.

The cost of going to university is much higher now than it has ever been and many children and their parents have taken out loans and stretched themselves financially to fund the programme. Research however shows that people with university degrees have a higher earning power than those that do not.

There are three deadlines (October, January and March) for university applications depending on the course your child is interested in applying for. All schools and colleges help their students with the process of application. It is also helpful for parents to engage with the process and help their children think through the courses that are right for them. Parents can help their children gather information and help them reflect on their personal statements (which need to be sent with the application form), visit the UCAS website ahead of time, help with searching for the universities that offer the courses of choice and help with planning some visits to universities. Universities usually send their prospectus on request.

Sex Education

Sex and Relationship Education (SRE): SRE is part of the national curriculum in schools and continues to be taught to children at various levels. Parents are able to withdraw their children from SRE lessons at school, but there is nothing to suggest that effective sex and relationship education encourages early sexual experimentation. In fact research conducted on behalf of the Department of Health (DOH) in 2000, showed that young people who have had good sex and relationship education at home and school, started having sex later in life and were less likely to have unwanted pregnancies and sexually transmitted diseases. It is important that children are adequately informed so they can make responsible decisions.

The legal age of consent to any form of sexual activity for females and males is 16 years old in the United Kingdom. It is however generally acceptable without legal consequences, for sexual activity to take place between two teenagers who mutually agree from ages 13 to 16. As discussed in chapter 3, health professionals can and do provide contraceptives and sexual advice to children under 16 provided they can justify that the child is mature enough to give informed consent and it is in the child's best interest.

According to the Family Planning Association (FPA), one of the charities concerned with sexual health, in spite of the availability of contraceptives, the United Kingdom still has the highest record of teenage pregnancy and abortion rates in Western Europe. The most vulnerable children include children of teenage parent themselves, those underachieving at school, those in the care of local authorities and those living in areas of high social deprivation. These categories include children who are likely to have low self-esteem.

Effective Sex Education: Many parents including Africans find it difficult to broach the issue of sex education with their children. They may feel they have little knowledge on how to approach the subject or that talking to children about it would lead to early experimentation or promiscuity.

There are several ways in which this can be best achieved. Parents could start by sharing their values and religious beliefs around sex with their children and why they hold such values and beliefs. They should give the children opportunities to share their views or comments. Parents should be prepared to listen and be careful not to lecture or use scare tactics. Children should be taught proper names for body parts from a young age and opportunities should be seized as they present themselves to explain or discuss a particular area. It also helps to understand what children are being taught at school and create opportunities to discuss this further at home.

It is important for children (8 to 11 years old) to begin to learn and understand human sexuality. Children from pre-teen years (10 to 13) should be made aware of the reasons and benefits for delaying sexual activity as well as getting appropriate advice on sexual health if needed. You can also borrow age-appropriate books from the library to aid the process of learning if you find it difficult to speak to them directly. There are many other strategies parents can use to approach the subject with pre-teens and teenagers such as those on www.mayoclinic.com.

Other Important Education Issues

Bilingual Children: The children of African immigrants either arrive with their parents, join them shortly afterwards or are born here in the United Kingdom. Many of these children are bilingual with English as a first language, while English is a second language for others. Some African parents refrain from speaking their African languages to their children, concerned that it may impede their understanding of English. Children can however learn two or more languages simultaneously without one affecting the other if the opportunity exists.

Having more than one language is more of an advantage than a disadvantage to anyone and many bilingual children have a better understanding of English literacy skills. African parents do not need to shy away from teaching their native language to their children. In fact, this should be encouraged, as a second language is likely to serve them well in future.

Many African languages are also at risk of extinction because they are no longer being passed down from one generation to the next. You could speak to your children in your African language in the home environment, while the children learn to speak English at school. Family members should be encouraged to do the same. It will require consistent effort on your part as parents; however with some patience and encouragement, you could be the proud parents of bilingual or even multi-lingual children.

Bullying in Schools: Being different and standing out from your peers can make a child more susceptible to bullying. A new student, one with special needs, a different accent or an African child in a predominantly white school setting can therefore be more of a target for bullies. It is normal for parents whose children are being bullied to feel emotional and be tempted to take the law into their own hands with some parents angrily confronting school staff, the bullies or the bullies' parents or encouraging the child to retaliate. Doing this is only likely to worsen the situation. Every child however has the right to feel emotionally and physically safe in school and bullying can and has been known to have tragic consequences.

Schools are required by law to have a written anti-bullying policy and procedures in place, which can be given to parents on request. It would therefore be helpful for you to understand how your child's school implements the policy. It is important that you reassure your child and stay calm, respectful but persistent when discussing the problem with school staff. Try to keep a record of incidents.

It is also possible that it is your child that is the bully. If this is the case, you must try to remain calm and not overreact. Bullies usually have underlying emotional issues that need to be addressed such as fear, anger and anxiety. Consider why he is behaving this way and work with the school and other members of your family in making the situation better. There are many situations that have been resolved with the school working with both sets of parents and children. There have also been situations when it is in one of the children's best interest to move to another school. Visit www.bullying.co.uk and www.kidscape.org.uk for more information and advice.

Catchment Areas: A lot of state schools use a priority admissions criterion called the catchment area. The catchment area of a school is usually an area within the locality of the school. This means priority will be given to the children living within that vicinity. Many parents are considering the schools in an area first before renting or buying property to increase their children's chances of getting into good schools.

Catchment areas are reviewed regularly and you should not assume that you are in a catchment area because you live within the vicinity of a local school. It is always important that you check with your local authority or the local authority of the school you are considering. It is also worth being aware that not all schools have the catchment area as a priority admissions criterion.

Clearing: Many A-level students pass their exams and get into the University of their first or second choice. Many others are disappointed when they find that they did not do as well as expected for either of the universities of their choice. A further option to getting into university after this is a process called *clearing*.

The student's results must still be reasonably good and he must be willing to be flexible regarding the choice of university and courses. The service is available shortly before the A-level results are published but most students use it after the results are out in August and they discover their results are not good enough for their choices. It is almost a 'first come, first served' process provided the student has already applied to UCAS, has not received any offers and the grades he has are good enough. It helps if parents are available when the results come out to assist their children with calls to possible alternative universities. It can be of added benefit to have other people helping as well.

For more information regarding universities visit www.ucas.com.

CHAPTER 9

Faith, Demonic Possession and Witchcraft

Faith and Spirituality

Faith and spirituality mean a lot to most Africans and are a major part of their daily lives. Generally, faith and spirituality, especially within African communities, are negatively portrayed by the media in the United Kingdom. The advantages and positive aspects of faith and faith groups are rarely mentioned. Christianity, for example is either portrayed as weak when it is not being vocal on certain issues or fanatical and offensive when it is. Islam is usually portrayed as violent and brash and people who practise traditional religions may be considered weird or strange.

Strength in Belief: There is little acknowledgement that many Africans have their social, psychological, emotional and sometimes financial needs met through their faith groups and have survived against all odds in the United Kingdom because of it. Many families are strong and well-established in their communities, retaining their belief in a brighter future because of the hope their faith gives them. It is rare to hear in mainstream media about the values, sense of belonging, strength, support and succour faith and spirituality give to many Africans which cannot be gained in any other way.

Faith and spirituality continue to be a pillar of strength, moral compass and the bedrock of the African community in the United Kingdom. Whilst many from the majority white population seek therapy and counselling, many Africans seek help from their faith groups and their God. Many people from different backgrounds including professionals are uninformed and fearful of what they do not know or understand about faith in the African community. The little that many know and have been trained on is contextualised in the negative aspects of faith and spirituality.

Most Africans who have a faith believe that the spiritual world has a great influence on the physical one, and believe that most physical events have their origins in the spiritual world. Whenever there is a misfortune in someone's life or family, there is therefore a tendency to attribute it to some happenings in the spiritual sphere.

Who Believes What: It is important to note that the degree of the belief and the way it is expressed differ amongst various faith groups and between individuals themselves. Whilst many faith groups believe the solution to a problem can be found in praying against the ill or evil without attributing it to a human being, some others believe there is usually a human 'agent' involved. Children, who may be seen as powerless and vulnerable, can then easily be targets and labelled as witches who are responsible for other people's misfortunes. The number of identified cases over the past few years in the United Kingdom, linked to witchcraft and spirit possession in the African community is relatively small, but the extent of the abuse in the cases identified has been particularly sinister, damaging and extreme leading to death in a couple of cases.

Victoria Climbie's abuse linked to witchcraft, which led to her death in the United Kingdom on the 25th February 2000, was unprecedented at the time it happened. It is unclear when her great-aunt began to abuse her, but she was reported to have believed Victoria was possessed by evil spirits and the ill-treatment Victoria suffered was part of the process of exorcism or deliverance as it is popularly called. Victoria later died from the extreme abuse meted out to her by her great-aunt and her boyfriend.

CASE 14 - DEMONIC POSSESSION & WITCHCRAFT

15 year old Kristy Bamu was tortured and killed on Christmas day, 2010 by his 28 year old sister, Magalie, and her partner, Eric, in their eighth floor London flat. Kristy and two of his sisters, 19 year old Kelly and 11 year old 'B' came to visit over the Christmas period from France where they lived, although the family originated from The Republic of Congo.

It appears Eric and Magalie believed the sibling group was possessed by evil spirits and witchcraft, called 'Kindoki,' the Lingala word for witchcraft. Kelly later reported during the trial that Eric and Magalie were fixated with the idea that the siblings were practising witchcraft and came from France to kill Eric and Magalie after an incident when Kristy bed-wet accidentally.

Shortly after the three arrived they began to be severely abused and tortured. Kristy was said to have been tortured over a period of four days with metal bars, a chisel, hammer and a pair of pliers in a prolonged ongoing attack. He was denied sleep and food and admitted to being a sorcerer, perhaps in the hope that the abuse would stop. Kristy was subsequently drowned in freezing water in the bath.

Making Sense of Kristy's Case: Any case like this is tragic. This one is particularly peculiar and disturbing for several reasons.

Firstly, the children had simply come from France on a visit. Eric and Magalie were not under a long-term obligation to care for Kristy, Kelly and 'B' in any way and they could have simply asked them to leave if they were uncomfortable with their presence. This did not happen. They seemed to believe that it was somehow their responsibility to exorcise Kristy and the two girls. It is unclear if and how much of a resistance the three children put up. Did they try to call for help or escape? Is it possible they simply deferred to Eric and Magalie out of an extreme form of cultural respect and fear?

Secondly, Eric who had a close relationship with the whole family and the children's father, Pierre, actually told Pierre in a telephone conversation that he believed Kristy was possessed by witchcraft and he (Eric) would kill Kristy if Pierre did not come for him. Kristy had also spoken to his father Pierre, over the telephone expressing fears that Eric would kill him. It is unclear how much Kristy told Pierre of the torture and beatings he and his sisters had already experienced at that time.

Thirdly, is the consideration of what an average parent would do if his son told him that he was being abused and believed he was going to be killed by his sister's partner? Another unnamed sibling was said to have manned the door while the torture was going on. Kelly and 'B' were said to have carried out the task of mopping up Kristy's blood after he was beaten. No one reported the abuse or sought help from anyone outside the family. Did the whole family believe to varying degrees in the possibility of a person being possessed by evil spirits or demons and how the person could be dispossessed, delivered or exorcised?

These are many parts to this case that remain unclear. Eric and Magalie were however found guilty and sentenced for Kristy's murder.

Vulnerability Factors: Certain factors may make some children more vulnerable to this sort of abuse than others. Children perceived as different, for example, defiant, strong-willed or disobedient children or those with an introverted personality or behavioural problems or disabilities such as attention deficient hyperactive disorder (ADHD), Asperger's syndrome, or autism could also be labelled as demon or evil spirit possessed.

In an attempt to resolve the problems they present with, they could be subjected to the emotional and physical abuse associated with exorcism or deliverance. The parents, community and leaders of the faith group they belong to may believe that subjecting them to deliverance services would cure or rid them of the demons.

Children in family settings where there is a likelihood of poor emotional bonding between child and carer and there is a belief in deliverance, may also be more vulnerable to being labelled as witches or demon or spirit-possessed. These include trafficked children, those in private fostering arrangements, those with a step-parent, those with a parent with mental health issues and those in families that attend places of worship where there is a strong belief that children can be possessed and can be delivered through means that can be considered abusive. In some instances it is the leader of the faith group who identifies the child as a witch or spirit-possessed, needing deliverance.

Abusive Behaviours: Many people, including Africans pray for and with a child and this can be a positive thing, provided the prayers do not include or constitute abusive behaviour. The process of deliverance carried out by some faith groups which would be deemed abusive include; shouting or screaming at the child, pushing and pulling, hair cutting, name-calling, beating, forcing the child to make a confession, long night vigil prayers, enforcing a fast or starving the child, forcing the child to drink concoctions of oil or urine, lacerations on a child's skin, sleep deprivation, threats of hell fire as well as varying degrees of isolation including being locked in a room.

It is important that parents ensure the place of worship they attend respects the rights of children and that the spiritual practice and any help they seek does not constitute abuse. Every place of worship for families in the United Kingdom must have an active child protection policy in place and a named person for child protection.

Every child should be seen as the collective responsibility of every adult around them and parents must remain vigilant for their own and other people's children. Values that protect children should be promoted. If you suspect a child is being labelled a witch or abused, please report your concerns to your local authority's children social services or if the child is in immediate danger, report directly to the police.

CHAPTER 10

Other Cultural Issues

Honour-based Violence

Also known as honour crimes, this is a crime committed against a member of a family to protect or defend the honour of the family or community they belong to. Although it exists in parts of Africa, it cuts across all nationalities and cultures and exists in various forms.

What makes it different from other forms of violence is the collusion with and approval of other family members or the community of the victim. It is usually a sign of male dominance where women must follow rules that are set mainly by the males within their culture. Women and girls are usually the victims and the aim is to control their behaviour or to punish them where it is believed they have shown disregard for the family's code of behaviour and therefore brought shame on them or the community. Females within the family have been known to aid and abet the crime and there have also been some male victims for example, homosexuals or those supporting the female victim.

Examples of honour-based violence include assaults such as acid attacks, mutilations and beatings, harassment and threats to kill, controlling sexual activity, forced abortion, forced marriage, kidnapping, false imprisonment and murder.

Victims have been severely assaulted and even killed for acts that may be perceived as minor misdemeanours to others, but which are considered as huge transgressions within that particular family and community. The acts may include having a boyfriend or having an affair, having an inter-racial relationship, being homosexual, seeking a divorce, refusing a forced marriage, dressing inappropriately or falling pregnant outside of marriage.

Many girls are still being forced to have abortions against their will in nearly all cultures till date. That is also a form of honour-based violence. Some parents from other cultures especially those from very closed communities may consider it a taboo, shame or dishonour that their children living in the United Kingdom want to deviate from their inherited culture albeit slightly on occasion and embrace aspects of a westernised lifestyle. It is families with these perceptions and extreme views that present as risks to committing honour-based violence.

The crime is difficult to detect as it happens behind closed doors with a code of silence existing between family members. Victims also find it difficult to come forward. Even when the violence leads to murder, family and community members have been known to mislead, obstruct and undermine police investigations.

Cases should be brought to the attention of the police and will be prosecuted under the specific offence committed; for example, common assault, inflicting grievous bodily harm, harassment, kidnap, rape, threats to kill and murder. They will also be recognised as honour crimes.

Forced or Arranged Marriage

A forced marriage is a form of honour-based crime. It can also be motivated by reasons other than honour, such as finances. It is one where one or both people do not want to get married but are made to do so against their will. An arranged marriage is different; it is where both parties agree freely to someone else (usually parents) identifying a spouse for them or assisting in the process and agreeing with the choice made.

A forced marriage is against the law in the United Kingdom, but an arranged marriage is not. The distinction can be difficult to recognise with the defining factor generally being the freedom of choice and how much of it either of the parties had at the time of the marriage. The validity of a marriage is questionable without the consent of one or both parties. Children as young as five years old have even been known to be married off without their consent or knowledge only finding out when they are older and are told they have to move in with a spouse who is a virtual stranger. Many others have been physically threatened, deceived, trapped and kidnapped into the marriage.

Although not common in Africa, as on other continents such as Asia, there are still a few countries where the practice is carried out. Similar to the practice of female genital mutilation (FGM) in this regard, girls resident in the United Kingdom have been known to be taken to their home countries on the pretext of a holiday or other function and then have their travel documents seized until the forced marriage has taken place.

Unlike FGM, male children have also been known to be victims of forced marriages. Some families have been known to force their homosexual children into marriage in the hope that this will 'cure' them.

Force, intimidation, manipulation, emotional blackmail, coercion, bullying, duress, pressure and undue influence are words that come to mind and a few, at least, are present in forced marriages as in Hadiza's story (see case 15). She went through a forced marriage in Egypt and came with her spouse to live in the United Kingdom.

CASE 15 - FORCED MARRIAGE

"I first met Omar when I was about 14 years old. He lived in our neighbourhood and although he was in his thirties and younger than my father, they were friends and he visited my family regularly. My parents would often sing his praises to me, telling me how kind and generous he was and how he had helped us with salvaging the family business, paying for the house, my brother's hospital bills etc.

I noticed my father always wanted me to be around when he visited and Omar would look at me in ways that made me uncomfortable. To my relief, he got a transfer at the company where he worked and travelled to the United Kingdom when I was about 16 years old. My father would however constantly tell me how much Omar liked and missed me and wanted me to come to the United Kingdom to live with him.

I knew they were planning to marry me off to Omar and I was often referred to as his wife. I didn't object as I didn't think I had a choice. He had helped with practically everything, and I knew I would be dishonouring the family if I objected. I however secretly nursed the hope that he would find someone he preferred in the United Kingdom.

I was 18 years old and Omar was 41 when he came back to marry me. My mother saw the frightened bewildered look in my eyes pleading with her not to let me go as we packed our bags to go to the United Kingdom. She tried to reassure me and whispered in my ear, "you will grow to love him, he's a nice man".

I didn't grow to love Omar and didn't have enough courage to leave him until I was 22 when I ran away with a young man I met at college. I left my two young children with Omar when I ran away. I really miss my children, but I feel free and happy, I also know I've brought shame on my family. I don't have the nerves to face Omar or my family yet, but I have to soon as I want to see my children."

Forced marriage is a violation of a person's human rights. The Forced Marriage and Civil Protection Act 2008 in the United Kingdom give courts powers to issue civil orders to prevent forced marriage or protect victims. Parents face up to a two-year jail term for contempt of court if they breach the civil order.

The government is currently proposing new laws that will make forced marriage an outright criminal offence instead of a civil one. While some organisations and people welcome the new legislation which will send a clear message to parents, others are of the view that the legislation could actually make the matter worse, deterring victims from coming forward as they will not want their relatives to end up with a criminal record. There is no current age limit for a victim of forced marriage and many young adults as well as children have been known to be victims.

There are huge social, cultural and emotional issues in forced marriages that could make it difficult for the victims to report. In spite of this, the Home Office in 2012 revealed that its forced marriage unit handles approximately 120 cases per month. The unit is dedicated to preventing British nationals being forced into a marriage at home and abroad and to assist anyone in the United Kingdom faced with the prospect of being forced into a marriage. There is more information regarding the activities of the unit and the help it can provide on www.fco.gov.uk/forcedmarriage, if you are concerned that a United Kingdom resident is being forced into a marriage. There is also a useful guide on their website for those who are already into forced marriages called the Survivors Handbook.

R-E-S-P-E-C-T

What does respect mean to you as an African parent? Africans in general strongly believe in the concept of showing respect especially towards their elders. Even in some cultures a sibling who is a year older can expect some deferential form of respect from the younger one and would have some corresponding responsibility towards him as the older child.

Some parents expect their children to demonstrate a high level of respect to them, as well as to other family members and friends as practised traditionally and historically in Africa, such as with greetings. This may include prostrating, genuflecting, stooping, kneeling, bowing or curtsying.

Many others are flexible, expecting their children to only show this when with certain older extended family members and friends. Some others cannot be bothered with any form of traditional ways of greeting or demonstrating respect. Many people believe you can be respectful without deferring to others in this way, while others feel it is an essential part of showing respect.

Many Africans especially West Africans believe it is rude to call an older person by their first name and to reduce the formality of using a title and the surname, such as Mr Jones or Mrs Jones, an older male is called brother, uncle or daddy and an older woman sister, aunt or mummy depending on their age and relationship.

Many children of African parents know to call their parents' African male and female friends uncle and aunty or add their first name to it, for example, 'aunty Sarah or uncle Sam'. Some African cultures still believe that avoiding eye contact with older people during a conversation is a sign of respect which many other people may find strange if displayed before them.

Giving or taking an item with the left hand can also be considered disrespectful in some parts of Africa. As in many areas, there is no right or wrong answer, one size does not fit all and many people do what suits them, their family and social setting best. It is however important that you share your values in this area with your children teaching them the why, how, where and when of this aspect of your culture.

What is vital is that children should display good manners, develop good social skills and learn to show respect to others in culturally acceptable ways.

CHAPTER 11

What Children Need

What does a child need to develop appropriately and have his welfare safeguarded and promoted? Many aspects of children's needs could be deduced from the previous chapters. Some factors discussed earlier such as the parents' immigration and employment status, housing, emotional stability and mental health can also impinge on a child's development and welfare. Below are some other vital factors required in meeting a child's needs. Some have been adapted from a popular assessment tool used in social work and called, *The Assessment Framework*.

Committed Carers: A child needs care and people to do the regular caring. Many would argue that this should ideally be a child's birth parents - indeed *both* birth parents. Parenting is a difficult task and more so when you are doing it alone without the support of another fully-committed adult

> *Parenting is a difficult task and more so when you are doing it alone without the support of another fully-committed adult who has an equal stake in the child's wellbeing.*

who has an equal stake in the child's wellbeing.

Several people will argue that the policies and laws in the United Kingdom over the years have favoured and encouraged single parenthood or motherhood and culturally in the United Kingdom, the role of fathers appear quite denigrated compared to what obtains in many parts of Africa.

Both parents have their own distinct contributions to the development of a child and the father's parenting role is not one that can be easily absorbed by the mother and vice versa. Some studies have even suggested that children with involved fathers have better educational outcomes, higher IQs and better linguistic and cognitive abilities. Not living with a child should not prevent a parent from being committed to the child's development and welfare.

More and more children in the United Kingdom are growing up in one-parent families which is fast becoming the norm rather than the exception. It is not a surprise that many children with behavioural problems usually have one parent missing from their lives. A high proportion of children in local authorities' care systems are also from single parent families.

Many children of single parents and those in step-parent families have however grown up to be successful, well-adjusted adults and continue to succeed against the odds. Nonetheless, it stands to reason that if single parenthood is an exception and not the norm, there is likely to be more support available to the children in those single parent families, both within the wider family setting and from community resources.

Needless to say, when a child is in other alternative care arrangements such as with private foster carers or the care of the local authority, the *commitment* aspect of the *care* may be compromised. When a child knows that he has carers who will watch out for him and are committed to his welfare, whether he lives with both of them or not, it gives that child a stronger sense of security and stability. Committed carers in a child's life provide a good foundation and make it easier for other aspects of that child's needs to be met.

Basic care: Every child needs his physical and daily needs met as part of his fundamental human rights. The provision of food, healthcare, shelter, clean and appropriate clothing, is not a privilege but a child's human right. Denying a child his basic needs should never be used as a form of discipline or punishment. Withholding a non-essential item and for example, luxuries that a child *wants*, rather than *needs*, may be considered as a form of discipline.

Family, Social and Peer Relationships: The value of this cannot be emphasised enough. No matter how good one or both parents are, the child needs other significant relationships which can help in his development and be supportive to him and the parents. Relationships with siblings and other family members are important in the development of cultural understanding, social skills and empathy.

Parenting in many parts of Africa can appear easier than in the United Kingdom because of the wide network of support available from other family members and the community. In most cases, African immigrants move abroad without taking their extended family members with them and it can be more difficult to make friends in a new environment and keep in regular contact due to the busyness of the western world. The benefit of a parent developing relationships with friends and available family members who can be part of the child's life is however, usually worth the effort.

As children mature, they spend increasing amounts of time with people their own age and age-appropriate friendships with peers become increasingly significant. Peers influence children's lives enormously and help them develop fundamental life and social skills. Making friends is not easy for all children and parents may need to tactfully support the process for children who find it particularly difficult to do so. Not all peer influences are positive and it is popularly said that, you are the company you keep. Parents may need to work with their children to ensure that the friends they keep are the appropriate ones.

Stimulation and Play: Play is not time wasting and unproductive as many people are inclined to believe. Many child psychologists actually believe that, play is the child's work. Play is an essential part of a child's development and crucial to a child reaching his full potential. Children need to play and in doing so explore and develop an understanding of how their environment and the world work. Some of the benefits of play which are unlikely to be gained in any other way include the following:

- *Building self-esteem*: As a child plays at what he is good at and becomes better at it, he realises he can actually achieve something significant without an adult being involved. This invariably builds his self-esteem and confidence.
- *Developing social skills*: As a child plays with other children, he learns how to share, manage conflict, earn respect and develop communication and assertion skills. He learns how to face and overcome challenges in making new friends whilst trying to maintain existing friendships.

Research also shows that children whose parents play with them develop superior social skills.

- *Being in Charge*: Play, allows a child to understand what being an adult is like. He realises during play that he can run a successful home or business on his own. Many parents can themselves remember playing at being a mummy, daddy or doctor. Play also helps with language development and gives the child the opportunity to work out his feelings on his own.

- *Developing other specific skills:* Modern day teenagers who spend a lot of time isolated or with only the internet for company should be encouraged to participate in play at their particular level. This could be in the form of attending structured leisure activities at youth clubs - tennis, athletics, football, dancing or learning to play a musical instrument. These activities can help them discover and develop new skills and talents.

Education: Many African parents value education and place a high premium on it, knowing it is a major key to a child making the most of his future. This is a good value for parents to have and to exhibit, as children are likely to develop core values similar to their parents.

Generally, there is a higher level of expectation in the United Kingdom for parents to become directly involved and participate in their child's education than in many parts of Africa, and there is evidence to show that children achieve better when their parents are more involved. It is therefore very important that parents try to build a good working relationship with teachers and other staff, get involved with their children's education, and participate actively whenever possible.

Parents should endeavour to read to their children and hear them read from a young age and this does not only have to be academic or school books. You can make reading fun and take turns to read notices and articles on trains, buses, newspapers and magazines.

As children grow older, parents should continue to show interest in their education, and try to make their role over the years as supportive and encouraging as possible. When considering educational achievement, try to stress progress and not perfection with your child, as the next stage in any challenge is usually easier than the ultimate goal. It is however important to remind your child that education liberates, enlightens and empowers, and it is one of the best ways to make the most of the opportunities available to him, as well as to distinguish himself, especially as a black person.

There is evidence to suggest that while some black children are doing very well academically in the United Kingdom of which children of African heritage constitute a significant majority, many more are under-achieving, failing to reach their potential, and are more likely to be excluded from school than their white peers for the same transgressions.

It is felt that the negative perception of each other that exists between black children and their teachers plays a significant role in this. Many black parents have also expressed concerns about being undermined by the school system.

Currently, there does not appear to be a national support group for black parents with regard to their children's education in the United Kingdom, but there are many local ones. You may need to search the local library or the internet for those available within your area or perhaps start a local one yourself. Advisory Centre for Education

(ACE) is a national charity that provides information, advice and support for all parents regarding children's education.

Emotional Warmth: Children need secure, stable and affectionate relationships with significant adults in their lives and there must be appropriate sensitivity and responsiveness to their needs. For young children, there is a need for appropriate physical contact, by means of comforting and cuddling. Research shows that babies who are not shown physical emotional warmth have delayed development. The good thing is that touching, cuddling, singing to babies and young children comes naturally to most parents, and must be encouraged.

As children grow older, many will continue to need some form of physical contact, such as hugs but it is also important to add taking out time to talk and listen, showing affection, a pat on the back, encouragement and praise, as part of emotional warmth.

There is a difference between praise and flattery. Think of what you want to praise and work on, being specific about it. This way the child remembers and is likely to repeat the positive act he was praised for in future. Parents must try to avoid sarcasm, put-downs, verbal abuse and negative humour. It is important that children have a sense of being valued and respected.

Identity: This relates to the child's growing sense of self as a separate and valued person. "Who am I?" "Where do I belong?" "What do I believe in?" - These are questions people unconsciously begin to ask themselves from adolescent years. Many children who grow up not knowing one or both of their birth parents struggle with aspects of their identity. Apart from that, children with an African heritage have the added challenge of possibly being bilingual, bi-cultural, practising a different religion and being different from their non-minority peers. While African parents should encourage their children to take pride in their heritage, they must also recognise that they are not just raising an African child but one with a new and evolving identity. It is important to understand that children are more likely to identify with the culture in which they are growing up.

A common problem in the child welfare field in the United Kingdom is when the child of an African immigrant learns about individualistic values, for example, rights, autonomy, individuality and independence from school, his environment and the mass media, and then brings these values home to a collectivist household environment where for example, responsibility, interdependence, family loyalty and affiliation are promoted.

Tensions often arise between parents and children who have grown up in different cultures and times. Negotiating and balancing perspectives, views and cultural values are not always easy tasks. African parents need to understand this and help their children growing up in the United Kingdom to develop a good sense of identity which incorporates both cultures. This is likely to be an ongoing process which can take some time to fully integrate or materialise.

African parents should be proud of their cultural identity and encourage their children to feel the same in relation to both their inherited and adopted cultures. The child's understanding and acceptance of both cultures play an important part in his self-image, belief in his own abilities, self-esteem and self-worth. Parents have a big part to play in making this happen.

Safety: Parents must do all they can to keep their children safe. Safety within the home environment includes keeping young children away from physical dangers. Medicines, lighters, matches, hot irons, hot kettles, bath tubs, domestic cleaning substances and other items capable of causing harm should be kept out of reach of young children.

According to The Royal Society for the Prevention of Accidents (ROSPA), accidental injuries are the most common cause of death in children over one year of age. Every year accidents leave thousands of children permanently disabled or disfigured and more than one million children under the age of 15 experience accidents in and around the home every year. Those aged 0 to 4 years old are the most vulnerable group.

Many accidents are preventable through increased awareness and improvements in the home environment. The law also makes it the responsibility of the driver of a vehicle to ensure children from birth until approximately 12 years old are kept safe when riding in cars by using the correct child restraints and car seats.

There are ongoing concerns that several pre-teens and teenagers are unsafe within their home environment being exposed to pornography and other materials on the worldwide web. The internet and modern mobile telephone technology are wonderful resources for accessing and sharing information as well as finding and keeping in touch with likeminded people. Children have however been exposed to explicit pornographic materials and been solicited and seduced by paedophiles pretending to be young people through the internet and there is an increase in threats and bullying through mobile telephone use. Over the past decade, many children have been tricked into sharing private information and explicit pictures of themselves and have become victims of bullying, as well as suffering physical, mental and sexual abuse, which were initiated over the internet.

Although more protection is available now than when the internet was first introduced, the threat of exposure to pornography and various forms of abuse remain and parents need to be vigilant. Remember that children are safest when adults know where they are and what they are doing.

The internet is a strange world to many parents, there is however still a need to know and discuss which sites their children are accessing and why. Computers, laptops and mobile telephones can all be fitted with filters and parental controls. You can also initiate conversations with children on keeping safe and emphasise regularly that you are available to help if they come across any inappropriate content.

There are many websites with information on keeping children safe on the Internet. The Child Exploitation and Online Protection Centre (CEOP), a parents' information website is one - www.thinkuknow.co.uk/parents .

Children should also be taught about personal safety from an early age. They should memorise the mobile numbers of their parents as well as their home address as soon as they are able to. They should be clearly and regularly instructed never to go off with strangers - whether adults or even with children like themselves.

As parents, you must ensure that any club or organisation they join has a child protection policy and the workers are vetted as suitable to work with children. Speak to and if possible, meet the parents of peers who host your children in their homes and ensure your children are happy with the arrangement before and after such visits.

While you do not wish to scare them or breed unnecessary suspicion, you want children to know that not all people can be trusted and that some people who appear nice, do actually harm children. Road accidents are the biggest single cause of accidental teenage deaths in the United Kingdom. Teenagers are easily distracted and prone to over-excitement especially when they are with friends; remind them to stay safe on the roads.

It is also a matter of great concern that some teenagers are becoming increasingly susceptible to street violence - with muggings, shootings and stabbings happening more frequently in recent years. When children are old enough to go out on their own, ensure you can reach them by phone. Work on developing agreements with them that clearly state that you at least, should know, *who* they are with, *where* they are going to and *when* they will be back home.

Guidance and Boundaries: Guidance, as in being a guide in itself pre-supposes that the parent has done what they want the child to do or been where they want the child to go and are now willing to show him or take him through the route of those journeys. By all means, teach your child; but as parents you must be prepared to demonstrate the values you want your children to exhibit.

Boundaries and limits should be set as they help keep children safe and secure. Remember that it is also natural and normal for children to test the boundaries by pushing or kicking against them from time to time. Work at ensuring that your boundaries or limits are reasonable. They must be neither so harsh that children cannot then develop their own sense of responsibility and independence nor so loose that they give little security or direction. As the parent, you must be prepared to stick to the limits you have set and be clear on aspects that are non-negotiable.

The ultimate aim is to enable the child to grow into an autonomous adult, holding his own values, aspects of which his parents have helped him develop, rather than being a clone of his parents or having to be solely dependent on parental rules.

CHAPTER 12

Tough Teen Issues

The teenage years can be described as the transition or metamorphosis years. Although the teen-age has generally been considered as starting from 13 to 19 years old, the psychological, biological and social changes associated with teenage years are starting much earlier in many children. Puberty, previously usually occurring in teenagers, is now starting in children as young as 8 years old.

Many parents complain about teenagers and probably find these the most difficult and challenging years in raising their children. Many people are however aware of the process of a caterpillar changing into a butterfly and parents can take some consolation in relating this with the process of a teenager evolving into an adult.

With patience, love, support and appropriate boundaries from parents, most teenagers come through the process fairly unscathed and transit to become responsible and independent adults. Many teenagers are better able to manage the challenges that confront them when they have good self-esteem, good friendships, success at school as well as in other activities. There are however some teenagers who stumble along the way and end up with some tough teenage issues.

Below are some difficult situations that teenagers may face and with which parents need to help.

Teenage Pregnancy: Many teenagers find it difficult to tell their parents that they are pregnant, fearing their anger and disappointment. It can also be very daunting and traumatic for a parent to find out their teenage daughter is pregnant or that their teenage son is about to become a father. If it happens, regardless of how you found out, you are likely to experience a range of emotions including anger, disappointment, fear, worry, anxiety and guilt. Remember that your teenager was probably anticipating an angry reaction from you if you are informed later rather than sooner. Try not to overreact by saying or doing something you will later regret; work at choosing your response and reaction carefully.

Your teenager needs you now more than ever and you should bear this in mind. Being able to communicate meaningfully with your teenager is very important at a time like this and while some questions and interrogations may be unavoidable, preaching or lecturing will probably not help. The participation of a mature neutral party you can trust can prove to be an immense support in being objective and helping you clarify your thoughts and emotions. This may well be, all her fault, but remember it is a mistake in her young life which she will have to live with and which will now change her life forever - whether or not she keeps the baby. Regardless of how she behaves, she is likely to be feeling stressed, ashamed, depressed and scared. She can no longer be the happy-go-lucky young girl, whose major thoughts centred on where to go and what to do with her friends.

The vital decision about what happens next - whether to keep or terminate the pregnancy needs to be made over the next few days or weeks. You need to ensure you get the right professional support for this and you may want to find other parents who have gone through this before.

Remember you are there to help and support your teenager, not force your opinion or use threats. It is her life and her body and while the decision she makes is likely to affect the whole family, it is ultimately her choice. Arrange to see your doctor immediately who should be able to refer you to local support services and clinics. You will be able to find more information and advice on websites such as www.brook.org.uk.

Drugs: Teenagers are generally tempted to experiment with new things and this, when coupled with peer pressure as research shows, results in up to 45% of teenagers male and female inclusive, trying drugs at some point. Some also use drugs as a form of escapism, perhaps from school or home pressures. The majority come out unharmed but for an unfortunate minority, the use becomes a habit or addiction.

Whether it is alcohol, cigarettes or hard drugs that your child is into, it is best to address the issue as soon as you become suspicious or find out. Signs such as, often asking you or other members of the family for money or stealing it, constantly chewing gum, poor personal hygiene, excessive tiredness, lack of interest in school or family, mood swings, loss of appetite and a desire to be alone may be indicators. As all drugs are addictive substances, it is unlikely the problem will go away by itself and it could even get worse without your involvement.

Obtain as much information as you can about drugs in general and the particular one you suspect your child is taking so you are speaking from a position of knowledge. Try not to lecture them but be clear about the risks the substance poses and your views. It is important that you still find grounds on which you can relate with your teenager and that you do not shut him off emotionally at this time, although it is equally important that you do not indulge him with money to feed the addiction.

Sometimes it could be a phase the teenager is passing through but it is essential that you seek external help if your suspicions and concerns grow. As in most issues regarding health, your doctor is a good first contact as they will be able to refer you to local services.

More information on drugs is available on websites such as www.talktofrank.com.

Gang Culture and Crime: The majority of United Kingdom street gangs are concentrated in inner city areas such as London, Manchester and Liverpool. Youth gang culture in the United Kingdom consists of youths from all races and there are many gangs in London and Manchester that consist of mainly black youths with some of them being of African origin.

Children join gangs for several reasons. These may include; craving a sense of belonging, excitement, recognition, money, respect and power over other people. The reality which many of them do not realise at the onset is that being in a gang makes them more susceptible to committing crime, dealing in or taking drugs, ending up in prison and being a victim of violence or even death.

Unfortunately, there are no current laws to prevent the formation and membership of gangs, but there are laws in place to prevent their criminal activities. The type of neighbourhood as well as the school a child attends may make him more susceptible to joining gangs and being involved in gang culture.

> *...there are no current laws to prevent the formation and membership of gangs, but there are laws in place to prevent their criminal activities.*

Male and female children as young as 10 years of age are known to have been recruited into gangs and used as mules to carry weapons and drugs for older members as they are less likely to be stopped and checked by the police.

There are many signs that parents should be aware of that could indicate that a child is in a gang such as a sudden loss of interest in school, staying out late without reason, a new nickname, possession of unexplained money or new items, parent or school becoming concerned about a change in behaviour, new friends, aggressive nature or a sudden change in appearance or dress style.

As with other negative situations, the best way to prevent children getting involved with gangs is to talk to them about it ahead of time and let them know the inherent dangers. It is also important for parents to affirm and praise their children, find time to be with them and be positive role models. Parents should encourage their children to be involved in activities such as sports or learning to play an instrument which can boost their self-esteem, channel their energy positively and prevent boredom.

If you find out that they are already involved in gangs, try to remain as calm as possible. It is always a good idea to ask appropriate questions and listen carefully, act in a composed manner and try to understand why they have joined, what activities the gang engages in and what alternatives there are to being in a gang.

Seek external help as soon as possible. Your management of the process could go a long way in determining the outcome. Find out if your child's school has a Safer School Police Officer attached to it or find out more information from your local neighbourhood police.

Depression: Some teenagers act out and have occasional bad moods and as a result, many people may be unaware that teenagers can be depressed. Circumstances such as parental separation, examinations, friendship problems, domestic violence or a death in the family can be triggers for teenage depression.

Depression usually twists one's way of thinking leading to negative perceptions, low energy and motivation. Although it is classified as a form of mental illness, the good news is that it is highly treatable and therefore it is important that help is sought as soon as possible.

One size does not fit all and the symptoms of depression in teenagers could manifest in various ways and range from: sadness or hopelessness, irritability, anger or hostility, tearfulness or frequent crying, withdrawal from friends and family, loss of interest in activities, changes in eating and sleeping patterns, restlessness and agitation, feelings of worthlessness and guilt, lack of enthusiasm and motivation, fatigue or lack of energy and difficulty in concentrating to thoughts of death or suicide.

The way depression manifests in adults is also different from how it manifests in teenagers which could make the signs easy to miss. For example, instead of showing sadness as some adults would, some teenagers could become very irritable. Some others could complain of unexplained aches and pains, be very sensitive to criticism or withdraw from some but not all people. Depression has led some teenagers to truant from school, become violent, take drugs, run away from home or even commit suicide.

There are many things that the parent of a depressed teenager can do to address the situation such as, learning about the condition and encouraging their teenager to do the same, encouraging the child to be socially and physically active and seeking emotional support for both parent and child. This can all be done alongside seeking support from your doctor. Medical doctors (or general practitioners) are able to refer you on to other forms of support such as a psychologist or psychiatrist. The treatment for depression ranges from various lifestyle changes to counselling, therapy and medication. Medication is usually a last resort and only used in extreme cases as a treatment for teenagers.

CHAPTER 13

Parenting Strategies

The majority of parents love their children and want the best for them, and discipline is part of the process of helping them develop into well-adjusted adults. Discipline can be carried out positively and does not have to be abusive.

Harsh and inflexible parenting styles can lead to relationship breakdowns between parents and their children whereby children become defiant, rebellious, suffer low self-esteem and some even end up in the care of the local authority and criminal justice system. Some parents have received cautions, criminal convictions and spent time in prison for child abuse, when in the view of the parents, they were merely disciplining their children physically.

Some children experiencing harsh, over-critical parenting, simply bide their time and leave home as soon as they are legally and financially able, sometimes severing all ties with one or both parents. Many others who have had very permissive and uninvolved parenting, display poor self-control, a low sense of personal responsibility and discipline which results in them being less competent than their peers and on many occasions they end up having problems with authority and authority figures.

Positive parenting includes praising and encouraging good behaviour, as children are likely to repeat actions they are praised for. It also includes teaching and training children on expected forms of behaviour as well as ignoring unacceptable behaviour *on occasions*, but helping them to understand, as they grow older, that actions have consequences.

This chapter will discuss some aspects of child development and some methods and strategies in parenting.

Understanding Misbehaviour

To work out a solution it usually helps to understand the problem. There are many reasons why children misbehave and these could include some of those described below.

First, parents may need to consider whether the child is misbehaving primarily because he has a legitimate unmet need. Remember the old adage, 'A hungry man, is an angry man?' The same is true of children. If you cure the hunger, the anger will be resolved. A baby for example may cry inconsolably if he is hungry, too hot, ill or wet and that cannot be considered misbehaviour. A toddler could also throw a tantrum because he is tired and sleepy or could run around to play on the streets as a need for stimulation or play and not because he is naughty or wants to annoy you. A teenager may want to spend more of his time with his friends than with family members as he used to a few years previously, and may get angry when prevented from doing so. This is a legitimate need for him and should not necessarily be considered as rebellion or 'going off the rails'.

Second, some behaviour is perfectly normal for a child's biological developmental stage. A teenager's brain is said to change rapidly once puberty hits and this can affect judgment or impulse control. Hormonal changes can also lead to problems which may manifest themselves as moodiness, anxiety or irritability. While this should not be an excuse for regular misbehaviour in teenagers, parents should be supportive and mindful of these changes and understand that the behaviour is likely to improve as they mature into adults.

It is normal for most toddlers to still bed-wet or wander off during shopping if not closely supervised as they are likely to be more interested in exploring their environment than in your shopping list. It is also perfectly normal for any child with little to occupy him, to find it difficult to sit still through a two-hour adult meeting. Always consider if your demands are reasonable for your child's age and level of development.

Third, children's personalities differ - even between twins. Each child is born with certain traits that underlie his personality. Some children are very amiable and compliant and may happily go along with whatever you ask them to do, while others will question or argue over every request you make of them or end up always having something to say. Some may be more defiant, self-absorbed, highly sensitive, and inattentive or introverted than others. It is important for a parent to recognise the child's personality and understand the most effective way to respond in order to bring out the best in the particular child.

Fourth, it is important to remember that children are children, and not adults being silly or trying to annoy parents. Children do not have many past experiences to learn from as they have never been adults before. They will therefore need to be taught, trained and shown how things are done –sometimes repetitively- including how to behave. It's also worth remembering that some children can have underlying problems that may need medical attention, for example, bed-wetting in older children. Children will also make many mistakes in growing up and learning, and parents should accept that making mistakes is a fact of life even as an adult. Parents sometimes call their children's behaviour naughty when it is simply an accident or a mistake that anyone could have made. A child can find it particularly distressing when his parents consider his mistakes a deliberate act.

Children are sometimes smacked or reprimanded for falling over or for accidentally breaking a mug which has slipped from their hands. As irritating or exasperating as some of these acts may be to adults, they are simply accidents to which children are more prone than adults.

While you may want your children to learn from your experience and direction, they will on many occasions learn by experimenting, and from their own 'trials and errors' and allowance should be made for this. For example, allowing a toddler to feed himself even though you know he is going to make a mess. When you can tell that an act is deliberate and non-accidental, it is always better to use the term 'unacceptable behaviour' than to label the child as 'bad' or 'naughty'.

Different methods of parenting will work for different children at different stages of their lives and you may need to adjust and change strategies as they grow. Below are some common approaches to parenting.

Developing Relationships

One of the things that can improve your child's behaviour is his or her improved relationship with you. The importance of developing a mutually respectful relationship with your child cannot be over-emphasised and is the bedrock for any other effective strategy. As you listen and take interest in what they are doing and feeling, your relationship with them grows positively and they are likely to want to make you happy as well.

One of the things that can improve your child's behaviour is his or her improved relationship with you.

A good approach to your relationship with a younger child for example, is to praise and encourage the behaviour you want and give him attention when he behaves well. Try to see things from your child's perspective and encourage their efforts when they make attempts to do things right.

Remember if your child thinks it is important, then it is important that you give it a similar priority. Find time to be with them and make listening and talking a regular part of your family life. Apart from one-to-one interaction, some families use family meetings to achieve this. Coming together on a regular basis and giving each member an opportunity to talk, air concerns, give compliments, praise, constructively criticise, or to reinforce household rules can make children feel they are a significant part of the household and that their opinion counts. You will not need to use too many strategies to discipline your child when you have a good mutual relationship with him especially as he grows older. Remember that any good relationship that exists is built on a foundation of time and effective communication.

Some parents believe the more informal they are with their children, the less respectful the children will be. Some fathers especially, believe they need to be stern, aloof and even feared. They feel if they let down their guard, their children will be rude and disrespectful, and there may be some truth in that. You are less likely to be fearful of someone who plays with you and whom you have fun with. It is however also true that you are also less likely to want to offend or upset someone you like being with and care about. If a child does not connect with his parents on an emotional level, he may comply out of fear for a while especially when the child is still young, but is more likely to defy boundaries, as he gets older.

The longest years of a parent's life with their child will most likely be when both are adults. This can become strained and distant in later years if the relationship was not well-developed when the child was younger. Developing a good relationship and communicating with your child regularly especially in their teenage years will take some time, energy and most of all patience on your part. Parents are the adults, and so the greater responsibility of building a good relationship here lies with them.

Modelling

James Baldwin, the African-American novelist, said;

> Children have never been very good at listening to their elders, but they have never failed to imitate them.

Parents must remember that they are always models for their children and are constantly being watched by them. They must therefore be prepared to exhibit the behaviour they want to see in their children as children imbibe more of what they see adults do than of what they hear them say.

The most significant values children will learn from their parents are what they see on a regular basis in the home environment. If you want your children to be kind, fair, show good manners, have good routines, have self-control, help with the cleaning and cooking, they are likely to do so if they see you doing the same. *Everything*, including eating habits, attitudes, work ethics, behaviour and manners can and is likely to be imbibed and emulated. That is why there are a higher percentage of children truanting from school who come from families where the parents show little value for education or have poor work ethics. It is probably also why obese parents are more likely to have obese children.

Prevention

There is an adage that says, an ounce of prevention is worth a pound of cure. Parents often foresee danger or disaster with regard to their children's behaviour and can take steps to prevent it before it occurs. Being proactive about this can prevent unnecessary stress on the whole family. So to prevent a tantrum with a toddler in a store, do not take them past the sweets or toys aisles. Do not lead them into temptation if you do not want them to fall into it. Do not leave the biscuit tin out if you do not want them to eat the biscuits. Use a night-time nappy for a toddler learning to potty-train. There is no evidence to suggest this will delay the process of the child becoming dry. It will simply prevent you from changing sheets and getting worked-up in the morning.

Pack items for school the night before, and plan some extra time into the mornings to prevent you running late and getting upset when children appear slow and stroppy. Take a story book, game console, colouring book, snacks, drinks or anything that can keep a child sufficiently occupied if you have to take your child with you to an adult function. Discuss chores with older children beforehand or write out a timetable and give them enough notice to do their allotted tasks. Asking them to wash the dishes or run an errand, on the spur of the moment while they are with friends or watching their favourite programme can be a recipe for disaster.

Planning ahead can save not only time and energy, but can prevent stress. Put out of reach or hide things you do not want young children to play with. Your planning ahead with this strategy in mind can make the difference between a day going smoothly or degenerating into chaos.

Establishing Routines

Establishing good routines help children feel more secure and confident. They begin to know what is expected of them from a young age and understand how to manage their time and behaviour. Routines may be different in each family but they still give children the same things - stability and confidence, reducing behavioural problems, teaching time-management and providing the child the opportunity to envisage what will happen next, a skill which, later in life, will be of great significance.

As you establish routines around bedtimes, bath times, mealtimes, chores, school mornings etc., your family life will be more peaceful. Even very young children understand routine and once it is well-established, will expect you to stick to it. For example, brushing teeth, taking a bath, changing into bedtime clothes, laying out clothes for the next day, praying or reading a bedtime story before going to bed will help a child begin to understand the importance of preparing for the next day and having a good night's rest.

A 2011 research carried out by YouGov for the Prince's Trust Youth Charity showed that young people who grow up without a daily routine such as regular bedtimes and set mealtimes are also more likely to under-achieve at school and suffer from low self-esteem.

The Disapproving Look

'Looks can kill!' is a well-known phrase. Many Africans were raised by parents whose disapproving look stopped any misbehaviour and put them on the straight and narrow path. The glance or glare of disapproval was enough for many, thereby obviating the need for the parents to say or do anything else. For many, it definitely spoke louder than words and discipline can be easier for parents and children who understand and use this effectively. This strategy can however leave children confused as to what they may have done wrong if they do not understand why the parent is giving the look of disapproval. They may also begin to attribute all their parent's negative moods to their behaviour and believe they are always at fault for them.

Many parents can themselves recall and identify with how the unexplained disapproving looks or negative moods of others around them have left them feeling confused and perplexed, wondering what they did wrong. It is unfair for your children to have to guess what it is they have done that you disapprove of. It is important that parents do not give out mixed messages when they are concerned about their children's behaviour and should be able to communicate this clearly to their children as needed.

Smacking

I have included this even though I have explained how it can be closely related to physical child abuse in chapter 4. Does smacking work in changing or modifying children's behaviour? It may do for a while, and it can be effective for young children, especially if they are close to danger and it is used appropriately on the bottom or palm of the hand.

It is however not advisable as a strategy for managing children's behaviour as it is against the law in the United Kingdom. However, as previously discussed, the law will deem it 'acceptable' if the smack is 'deemed reasonable'. Even many childcare experts think that the law regarding smacking of children by parents in the United Kingdom is confusing and should be clearer. As on the one hand it is against the law, on the other hand, a parent can get away with it if the smack is considered reasonable; some feel it should be a clear, yes - smacking is lawful or no - it is not; with no exceptions.

The confusion appears to continue with the fine line between what is considered reasonable or unreasonable being ambiguous for many. It is clear however, that many parents overuse smacking for very minor misdemeanours, mistakes or accidents - even in public places. Some go further than a light smack on the bottom or palm of the hand and resort to pinching, ear pulling and slapping across the head and face.

Many parents resort to smacking when they are stressed and angry with their child and for many it has become a difficult habit to break. It suggests therefore that the act can be more about the parent's anger than the discipline and correction of the child. There is also a higher likelihood of accidental injury when smacking is used. For example, you may plan to smack the child's hand, but the child's sudden movement means you hit his face instead. The child can therefore come to more harm than intended.

A government survey on parents in 2007 showed that smacking is becoming a less commonly used form of discipline as more parents recognise that there are more effective and acceptable methods of disciplining children. Whilst many parents say they will not smack, a majority of parents however say that smacking should not be banned outright. Many organisations advocate and support legislation to ban smacking. The survey showed that around half of parents think it is sometimes necessary to smack a child, and many say they have smacked at least one of their children.

Another disadvantage to smacking is that it leaves many parents feeling guilty and apologetic, which invariably turns the attention away from the child's behaviour to theirs. Children, especially older ones, may in addition, feel embarrassed, angry, defiant and hurt, lose some self-esteem, retaliate, and not necessarily feel corrected. Remember that smacking can take the focus off the unacceptable behaviour and the discipline and correction intended are then lost.

As fewer and fewer parents use this method, your child is also likely to see himself as being treated differently from his peers. Your strategy for discipline may then be deemed abusive by your child and others. Research also shows that children who are physically punished and smacked are more likely to behave aggressively in schools.

Childcare professionals actively discourage smacking as a method of discipline and there is pressure from organisations and other European countries for the United Kingdom to remove the indirect smacking law here. It is against the law for childcare professionals such as childminders, nursery nurses and teachers to smack other people's children in their charge.

Overall, there has been no measurable long-term benefit derived from smacking and other forms of corporal punishment as compared to a loving, firm, alternative parenting approach without it. There may appear to be some ambiguity as to what the law allows or not. What is however clear is, the law does not permit anyone being deliberately or recklessly cruel to a child or causing injury to him as an act of discipline.

Shouting

Many parents speak firmly, sternly or shout at their children and this can work to stop unacceptable behaviour or act as an effective deterrent from danger. 'Stop it!' or 'Don't do that!' are phrases commonly used by parents. Again, there is a fine line between speaking in a stern, firm voice and shouting.

Shouting loudly at a child can be scary, intimidating and very frightening, especially for young children. The intention to discipline and correct the unacceptable behaviour could be lost if they feel intimidated and scared. Shouting can also suggest to your children and others around you that you are aggressive, have actually 'lost it' and that you are out of control or unserious, particularly if this is a method you use often.

Children are likely to model your behaviour as discussed earlier and shout back as they get older and the whole purpose of correction is therefore lost as you both shout back and forth. Instructing a child with a stern, firm voice should not include verbal abuse. Practice telling your children what you want them to do and not just what you do not want them to do. Focusing on the positive makes a big difference.

Negotiating or Bargaining

Parents need to be firm and consistent. It should however not be the same as being rigid. Although quite foreign to many African cultures, negotiation as a child-rearing technique can be an effective strategy in helping you maintain fair discipline without appearing weak. Children may want to negotiate longer bedtimes for example, on weekends or special occasions and it is healthy to consider and bargain for an agreeable time when they propose it.

It is not about winning or losing but about coming to a reasonable agreement. It is a good way of developing social skills in children as they begin to see how negotiations work in relationships. Like all strategies, this method will not always work and there are times when negotiation cannot be an option or a child is too young to understand it, for example, where health or safety issues are concerned.

Overall, do not forget that you are the parent, still in charge and still able to make the final decision.

Offering Choices

The freedom to choose makes us all feel empowered and everyone likes being able to make choices. When children are given choices, it not only empowers but communicates adult respect of them. Choices can aid compliance, better behaviour and help minimise conflicts between parents and children. It is a step in growing up when you begin to give them the opportunity to influence the situations they are in to an extent.

Making choices is a skill that children will need to have and use for the rest of their lives, so it is good practice for them in deciding what their preference or what they believe the best option for them is. It also aids responsibility and independence. It is usually best for parents to pre-plan and first decide what choices to allow the children to make as you inevitably give up some control as a parent when you allow them to choose.

Try to give children only two or three choices at a time to prevent them being confused and indecisive and ensure you are able to meet your obligations. For example;

- *"Will you like to play on your game console or read a book?"*
- *"Will you like cereal or toast?"*
- *"I need you to help out today; will you vacuum-clean or do the dishes?"*

Give them enough time to consider the choices before them and remember that you have allowed them to choose and should not later withdraw the choice the child has made.

Telling-Off

There is nothing wrong with showing your displeasure and telling your child off for unacceptable behaviour. You should however observe some rules in doing this.

Firstly, address the behaviour, not the child, so there should be no name-calling or verbal abuse.

Secondly, tell the child what he has done wrong and what you want him to do now or the next time. This should therefore not be another opportunity for non-stop nagging.

Thirdly, do not overuse this method; move on from the incident as soon as possible and try to restore your relationship to normal.

It is important not to let it fester or ruin the day. If a sanction or further discipline is needed, perhaps because the child has not heeded previous warnings, let him know what it is and move on from there.

Threatening

Many parents threaten their children as a method of compelling them to behave better and have achieved some results this way. Threatening is however usually done in anger and on the spur of the moment without thinking its consequences through properly. Parents are then left with the choice of maintaining their credibility and carrying out their irrational threats, or risk not being taken seriously by failing to follow through with the threat.

Threatening does not always encourage cooperation and may actually encourage defiance, especially in strong-willed children who may want to see how far they can push the set boundaries and end up provoking the parent further. Some African parents sometimes threaten to send their children back to Africa or throw them out of the house.

Very few carry out these threats and those that do not, lose some credibility with their children who see them as all mouth and no action.

A few parents have resolved to carry out the threats to take their children back to harsh, boot camp like situations, which have led to child protection concerns. It is important to note that many children are actually sent back to Africa for reasons other than discipline. This has worked out as an opportunity for a lot of children to develop an understanding of their heritage, culture and language as well as getting to know relatives they would otherwise have never met.

CASE 16 - THREATS

A mother was jailed recently for taking her 17 year old son to Nigeria and refusing to bring him back to the United Kingdom at the court's order. Edirin Idogun came to the United Kingdom from Nigeria in 2004 to live with his mother Lydia Erhire. He became a United Kingdom resident, but in 2010 his mother sent him back to a Nigerian boarding school.

It appeared she had ongoing concerns about his behaviour and relationships with people she considered 'unsatisfactory'.

Edirin had clearly been concerned about his mother's threats to return him to Nigeria in the first instance and sought help from an organisation. He apparently raised concerns about being forced into a marriage against his will in Nigeria and the court issued a protection order under forced marriage laws and provided him with emergency accommodation.

His mother sent him to Nigeria on what appeared to be a holiday shortly after the court order was made, but he did not return to start college in the United Kingdom in September 2010. Instead, he was sent to a Nigerian boarding school to start his A Levels.

Edirin claimed he was subjected to beatings and exorcism in Nigeria to purge him of his disobedience. The courts ordered Lydia to bring him back, but she was said to have obstructed efforts to ensure this was done and was subsequently jailed for eight months.

Time out or Grounding

Most children will accept their parents' boundaries out of love and healthy respect and on most occasions will adhere to you withdrawing their liberty by grounding or keeping them still for a period of time. The purpose of this is three-fold - it shows your displeasure; gives them an opportunity to think of their unacceptable behaviour; and prevents them from enjoying the freedom of movement they would otherwise have had and enjoyed.

Some parents will already be aware of what appears to be a Euro-centric method of discipline which is using time out for young children by making them sit on the stairs or in a corner to think over their behaviour for a set period of time, depending upon their age.

However this is also very common in many parts of Africa with different areas having their own variation of it. Many parents of African origin will recall having to stand in a corner of a room, facing a wall or being made to sit under a tree while their peers were running around and doing some other exciting activities.

It works with young children, whose freedom of movement can be restricted for short periods provided you are prepared to enforce it consistently and appropriately. It can also work with older children by preventing them from outdoor activities or from spending time to be with their friends. Grounding or time out may not work with some children with extreme or defiant behaviour patterns, or with introverted children who already love their own company and would not mind being isolated for long periods of time. If the parent feels this strategy is ineffective or feels unable to enforce it, the next suggestion may help.

Withholding Privileges

Withholding privileges can work even with older children. If your teenager knows his pocket money will be reduced, he will not get credit for his mobile phone or he will not be allowed to use the car if he does not keep within certain boundaries, he is likely to comply as he would probably place great value on the convenience of making calls from his phone, or the privilege of having more money for leisure or using the car.

The truth is, withholding privileges works even with most adults. It is one of the reasons why people drive within speed limits and park in appropriate places. Most adults do not want the privilege of driving withdrawn from them or to lose their hard-earned money paying fines; they want the convenience of driving a car. They would rather toe the line than endure having their car towed away.

More and more parents use this with older children when other methods do not work. It is a rare child who will not miss having his favourite gadgets, pocket money, the use of the car or the privilege of whatever else is important to him being taken away for a period of time.

Indulging Children

Everybody enjoys being pampered; spoiling or indulging your children occasionally will not harm them. It could even help your relationship with them if they remember occasions when you have been extra nice. However, if this is done too often, you may end up with spoilt children.

There are perhaps very few things as annoying, stressful and off-putting as a spoilt child. Spoilt children can have an exaggerated sense of entitlement, blame others for their own actions or refuse to accept no for an answer. Some do not experience any guilt about how other people feel as long as they get their own way and find it easy to hurt their parents or other people. Spoilt children can be frequently rude and lack manners, displaying poor social skills and end up being unable to make friends or keep the ones they do make.

Some parents let their children get away with everything and dance to all their children's tunes. If you over-indulge your child and do not set appropriate limits, your child may begin to think the world revolves around him. You will also be setting him up to fail if he cannot display good social skills, graces and consideration for others in a society where getting ahead in life is based on such values. Prioritise your children, but do not sacrifice everything else in doing so.

Like everyone else, children will sometimes be unhappy, angry, not always get what they want or suffer the consequences of their actions. While you may ignore unacceptable behaviour on occasions, especially when they are younger, let them understand that rudeness, lacking manners and being inconsiderate of others are unacceptable.

Remember as a parent, the buck stops with you and it is your duty to make the final decision as long as you are not being abusive.

Relax and Enjoy Them

Parenting is not always an onerous role, as most parents know. It has its many advantages, and can be fun and enjoyable. Children can be witty and funny and you can also learn a lot from them. Most children grow up to be healthy happy adults who enrich the lives of their parents as great friends, support and companions for many years to come. Once they are grown, you are likely to miss those years and reminisce on those cartoon characters they loved whose names you can now only vaguely recall.

A good relationship and firm consistent love are the keys; use disciplinary methods sparingly. Model the behaviour you want to see, listen to and talk to them, let them choose sometimes, plan ahead to prevent disasters, establish good routines and enjoy them before they leave the family home and the next generation comes along.

The ideas mentioned above are just a few of the strategies parents adopt and there are many others. Many African parents have been brought up themselves by parents who have never used some of these strategies and may find it difficult initially to discipline their children in this manner. It may take a while to embed some good approaches, but practice, persistence and consistency will eventually pay off.

CHAPTER 14

Take Care of Yourself!

A lot of parents in today's world are stretched, juggling many balls in the air and are sometimes close to breaking point. Many African parents have stressful jobs, hectic lifestyles and face increasing demands and obligations on them both at home and abroad. Some parents who have physically abused or neglected their children are neither hardened criminals nor mentally ill. Many are lonely, unhappy, oppressed, abused, angry adults under heavy stress trying to manage many roles and end up doing things they should not. Stress is an emotional and physical response to pressures from the outside world, and seems more pervasive and persistent today than ever.

Numerous studies have shown that between 75% to 95% of all visits to the doctor are stress related. De-stressing and taking care of yourself are therefore parenting strategies and can serve as preventative measures against negative parenting traits.

How do you look after yourself? Many parents will have answers to this already. De-stressing and looking after yourself will mean different things to different people. Visit a spa or take a day off to rest if and when you can. If you can afford to, take a weekend break. Learn to say no to requests and commitments that are less than essential when you have too many demands on your time. Whenever you begin to feel guilty when you say no or when you are doing something for yourself, remind yourself that you are taking 'me-time' and deploying an effective parenting strategy! An African adage says, 'It is not the wings but what a bird eats, that gives it the ability to fly.' Translated, this simply means you need the right amount of emotional and physical energy to fulfil your roles in life appropriately.

Whatever you do, what is important is that it helps you feel relaxed, refreshed, re-invigorated and strengthens you to continue with the challenges of parenting and the other demands in your life. Below are some stress relievers and healthy lifestyle habits.

Eat Right: One of the primary ways of taking care of yourself is by eating a healthy, balanced diet. A healthy diet offers your body the energy and nutrition that it needs to function properly. African foods can be very tasty and nutritious but some can also be high in fat and calories. Many adults in the United Kingdom are becoming obese or overweight, which means they are eating more than their body needs or they are eating the wrong things. Many people eat mindlessly, satisfying their hunger without considering what they are putting into their bodies.

Eating a diet high in fruit, vegetables and grains can help with managing your weight and also reduces the risks of developing certain diseases and helps protect against others such as stroke, heart disease and some types of cancer. Some grains and vegetables are high in fibre which can also help to prevent constipation.

According to the National Health Service (NHS), eating a diet based on some starchy foods such as rice and pasta, plenty of fruit and vegetables, some protein-rich foods such as meat, fish and lentils and some milk and other dairy foods; whilst cutting down on fats, salt and sugar, will give you all the nutrients you need.

Be mindful of your portion sizes, junk food and snacking between meals. It could also help your digestive system to eat heavier meals earlier in the day and lighter ones later.

Sleep Well: While most of us do not understand the scientific reasoning behind sleep, everyone sleeps and many are aware of the benefits of sleep to our general wellbeing. Insufficient sleep can make one feel irritable and moody while getting a good night's sleep can make you feel ready to take on the world and the many challenges it presents. Numerous studies have also shown that there are more significant benefits to sleep than merely affecting our moods. Sleep plays a vital part in promoting physical health, longevity and mental and emotional wellbeing.

A good night's sleep will not only make you feel better, but will make your thoughts clearer and your emotions less fragile. Many adults cut down on sleep in today's high-paced society so they can catch up with other demands. The truth however is that enough sleep is needed to make the other hours effective and productive.

If the limited sleep persists, it can lead to long-term mood disorders such as anxiety or depression and increase the risk of developing certain types of diseases such as colon cancer and high blood pressure. Without adequate sleep, our body also has a difficult time healing and repairing itself from damage. Adults differ in how much sleep they need individually, which for most people will range from six to nine hours. The major test of enough sleep is your level of alertness when you get up and during the rest of the day.

Parents of young children who wake up during the night, or those working shift hours may find it particularly difficult to get the required hours of sleep at night. It is advisable for nursing parents to take short naps with their children during the day when they can, as naps can also help to keep you refreshed, renewed and more focused. Work on keeping a consistent sleep schedule, leaving unfinished activities till the next day. Alcohol, nicotine and caffeine are known to disturb sleep and are best avoided at night. Make your bed and room as comfortable and uncluttered as possible. Remember, the benefits of sleep cannot be gained any other way.

Walking and Other Forms of Exercise: Many parents shut their ears and minds when they hear the word exercise as they begin to picture some back-breaking routine. You do not have to go to a gym to exercise and many people who have paid large amounts of money to gymnasia have not attended beyond the first few weeks.

The key to effective exercise – whatever activity you choose to do is *consistency*. Therein lays the power and the benefit. Exercise could simply mean regular swimming, dancing, jogging and playing an energetic sport such as table tennis or brisk energetic walking.

> *Every able-bodied person walks, it is doing enough of it in a day that counts as exercise.*

Walking is considered one of the easiest and best ways to keep active. The 'I am too busy' or 'I don't have time' maxim is also not an excuse for forgoing walking. Every able-bodied person walks, it is doing enough of it in a day that counts as exercise. Walking can help clarify your thoughts, give you more energy, help your posture and tone your body. Walking also makes you feel fitter, help with weight control, make you feel more relaxed at the end of the day and aid good sleep. Even people with diagnosed depression claim they feel better when they incorporate walking in their treatment programme.

It can be the first thing you do for the initial half hour after your spouse walks through the door, if you are a stay-at-home mum with a young child. If you are single or have older children who cannot be left alone but do not want to come with you, you can arrange childcare with a trusted friend or neighbour with whom you can exchange walking times.

Most working parents get lunch breaks and part of these can be used to walk. You can also use the stairs instead of the lift at work or railway stations or get off a station or couple of bus-stops before the one closest to your home and walk the rest of the way. It can be done, even with enjoyment, if you set your mind to it. A half-hour walk four times a week, will have amounted to, two hours of consistent and meaningful exercise in a week.

Get Help: Many parents are filling many roles and sometimes it is simply too much to do the cooking, shopping, washing, cleaning, ironing, gardening, school runs, reading bedtime stories, attending school meetings and going to work all by yourself on a regular basis. Some help even if just occasionally, can make a big difference.

There are many adults and teenagers who can be paid to do a few hours of cleaning, gardening or ironing. You can enlist the help of your older children and delegate some household tasks to them. Some close friends, neighbours or relatives may also not mind being asked to help with baby-sitting or the school run when they can. Many parents now do their grocery and other shopping online from the convenience of their home instead of driving around or going on buses with heavy shopping. Pay for someone to help you as regularly as you can afford to. Remember, you are not superman or superwoman.

Other Relationships: Take time out to attend to your other significant relationships on a regular basis, and make time to develop some if you do not have them already. This is especially important for couples. It is easy to lose sight of each other as you focus on meeting the needs of your children and maintain other parts of a hectic lifestyle.

You may want to set up a date night on a regular basis with each other. It may feel artificial at first, but could be the key to strengthening your relationship. Many marital relationships have broken down because couples gradually grew apart; neglecting each other, while focusing on child-rearing and other pursuits.

You will also need to develop other significant relationships individually. If you are a single parent, take time out to be with your friends regularly. People with a good social circle have more fun, have more support in times of crisis and lead less stressful lives. You will definitely need your other relationships, especially as your children grow older and want to spend more of their time with their own friends.

Avoid Excessive Competition: Many African parents in the United Kingdom work hard and are highly driven to succeed. This is a good thing on one hand, and no one can deny that financial freedom and career success are good and important. However on the other hand, many do not know when to stop or how to balance competing demands appropriately.

Success, if not placed in the right perspective, can become an insatiable desire and a never-ending unreachable goal. The drive to succeed can lead to unhealthy competition and relationship breakdowns as parents work even harder and longer, ignore their families and start comparing themselves to others. Excessive competition and comparison have led many people to literally bite off more than they can chew - acquiring what they do not need, just to impress people who do not necessarily care about them, all to the detriment of those that really matter. It is not just a problem amongst Africans, it is a twenty-first century problem, and you may have heard of workaholics who cannot take a break.

Unfortunately, many people are only forced to take a break when they have a breakdown in their relationships, body or mind. It is important to set goals, but goals must be realistic considering the impact on all the other important relationships and demands on parents. We must remember that the most important things in life cannot be measured in monetary terms. Bear in mind the oft quoted phrase that, "real life is not measured by how much we own."

Lighten up: There are pressures of twenty-first century living all around us and life in the United Kingdom can also have its challenges especially for an African immigrant. Some people can however be more highly strung than others even when undergoing the same situation. Everyone can find pleasure and laughter in the little things of life.

The happiest people are not necessarily the richest; having a sense of humour, even in troubled times can help tremendously. Learn to laugh often with and without your children and try not to take too much to heart. Laughter has more benefit than we give it credit for. A cheerful heart is good medicine. This has been proven to be true scientifically. Laughter provides a physical and emotional release that takes the focus away from the pressure, anger, guilt, anxiety or whatever your current life challenge is.

A good belly laugh exercises the diaphragm, contracts the abdominal muscles and even works out the shoulders, leaving muscles more relaxed afterwards. Laughter provides a good workout for the heart, reduces the level of stress hormones like cortisol, epinephrine (adrenaline), dopamine and growth hormone. Laughter also increases the level of health-enhancing hormones like endorphins, and neuro-transmitters - the number of antibody-producing cells and enhances the effectiveness of T cells.

All these mean a stronger immune system, as well as fewer physical effects of stress. Find things that will make you laugh. Watch a comedy - even one you have seen before. Call a friend and reminisce about old times. It has been said that angels can fly because they take themselves lightly. Learn not to take yourself too seriously - and, above all, learn to laugh at yourself.

Pray: Many Africans in the United Kingdom believe in God and belong to a faith group. For them reading the scriptures, meditation and prayer are great de-stressors. Spending time with and focusing on a greater source of strength and help who many believe can do anything and change any situation can make a big difference, mentally, psychologically, emotionally and spiritually. It reminds many of their humanity and limitations and makes them feel they can relinquish the care and burden they carry to a God whom they believe has the strength to take over from where their own strength ends.

Prayer has been called the speech of heaven and an opportunity to show gratitude and share all aspects of life with God. To pray is to live beyond the narrow walls of the self and acknowledge a greater source of control. Prayer has helped many people deal with anxiety and given them inner peace.

CASE 17 - PRAYER

This is how Kolitzwa described her experience:

"It had been a difficult week. Money was tight as Jairo (husband) had still not found work after his last contract ended. We had to send money back home to pay for my mum's medical bills and Jairo's younger brother's school fees. We also had a backlog of unpaid bills.

Victoria (16 year old daughter) had fallen out with her friends; she's melancholic and taking it out on all of us at home. Richard (13 year old son) came home with a ripped school blazer and admitted that he had lost his already overdue library book. I came in even later than usual from my job as a social worker. I had to deal with a crisis. A service user on my caseload had committed suicide. I felt I had no more energy to deal with the issues of life. I kicked off my shoes and lay down on my bed in the dark thinking about all these problems or issues as I now refer to them.

I decided to turn my focus to God. I believed He was present in the room with me. I poured out my heart in prayer asking for peace, strength, wisdom and provision. I remembered that I had read in the scriptures, that I would pass through fire and not be burnt. A peace and joy I couldn't explain began to spring up from within me. A hymn came to mind, *Great is thy faithfulness*, and I started singing in the dark, then, another one, *It is well with my soul* and I sang that too. I began to think of and became thankful for all the things going well. We were all healthy, we had each other, the children were doing well at school, my job was still stressful but I loved what I did and had very supportive colleagues. Besides, we had been through worse and came through just fine. Somehow I knew everything was going to be alright.

I got up after about twenty minutes to eat some dinner, still singing my songs. I had not seen the answers to all my prayers and questions yet - but I felt stronger. I had faith and I had hope."

The Future is Now: Many African immigrants eventually return to their countries after a period of time in the United Kingdom, but several others choose to stay. Many that choose to stay have naturalised as United Kingdom citizens and for them the United Kingdom is no longer a place they have come to work, live and raise children - it has now become home and their country. Many have integrated well into the system and adjusted part of their inherited African culture to meet their needs and those of their families. They recognise as others have done that culture is not stagnant, it is an evolving phenomenon.

The Africans who return to their home countries after several years are often surprised that they have also changed unconsciously and adapted in numerous ways to the culture in the United Kingdom and have to somewhat change and adapt to their home country again. Change as it is said, is the only constant thing in life. Also, one cannot apply yesterday's rules to today's challenges, we therefore have to wisely adapt to society as it exists today and in the place we find ourselves.

Do your best and remember that there is no perfect parent and no one always gets it right. Enjoy the years of your children being with you and take lots of pictures whenever you have the opportunity, and in these days of technology, you have no excuse to neglect this. As you make some changes and adapt to your new environment even in your parenting role, you will begin to see the benefits for you and your children.

Overall, remember that time flies, childhood years do not last forever and can never be re-captured. Most of your children will be grown and out of your nest sooner than you think.

ACKNOWLEDGEMENTS

No one achieves anything of significance alone and I am highly indebted to more people than can be mentioned here. I must however acknowledge and say a special thank you to:

- Bukie Williams for enthusiastically providing the emotional and financial support needed to start and complete this work and aiding the process to discover, develop and deploy this part of me.
- Fewa Williams and Eri-ife Williams, for giving me the opportunity to practice raising children with a dual identity and culture.
- Dr Tayo Adeyemi, for teaching and motivating me for many years and modelling great courage in adversity.
- Dr Kola Munis for reading and contributing to the first few pages I called a manuscript and for encouraging me that this is a much needed work.
- Winsome Collins and Feargal Brady for providing insight and suggestions from a social work perspective and for not being too busy to help.
- Dr Claudia Bernard and Anna Fairtlough of Goldsmiths, University of London for taking time out of a hectic schedule to read and comment on the work.
- Mr Seyi Obakin, Centrepoint UK, for his superb review and comments.

- Toks Williams, Kola Olutimehin and Teena Adande-Enahoro for excellent editorial and proof-reading work and for going far beyond the call of duty.
- The trustees and volunteers of Yeshua's Arm, my friends and ex-colleagues who shared my passion and each played a part in ensuring, African Parents Must Know!

BIBLIOGRAPHY AND REFERENCES

AFRUCA (2009); *What Is Witchcraft Abuse?*

Beckett, C., 2007; *Child Protection: An Introduction. London:* SAGE.

Bernard, C. and Gupta, A., (2008); Black African Children and the Child Protection System. *British Journal of Social Work.* Vol. 38 (3), p476-492.

Corby, B. (2000); *Child Abuse: Towards A Knowledge Base.* Oxford: OUP.

Department For Children, Schools and Families (DCSF) (2007); *Review of Section 58 of The Children Act 2004.* [pdf] London: The Stationery Office.

Department For Children, Schools and Families (DCSF) (2010); *Working Together To Safeguard Children.* London: The Stationery Office.

Department of Health (DOH) (2000); *Framework For The Assessment of Children In Need and Their Families.* London: The Stationery Office.

Kirshenbaum, M. and Foster, C., (1991); *Parent/Teen Breakthrough*: Plume.

Kübler-Ross, E. (2005); *On Grief and Grieving: Finding the Meaning of Grief Through the Five Stages of Loss.* Simon & Schuster Ltd.

Samlin, N. and Whitney, C., (2003); *Loving Without Spoiling: And 100 Other Timeless Tips For Raising Terrific Kids.* McGraw-Hill.

Nelsen, J (2006); *Positive Discipline*: Ballantine Books.

NSPCC (Updated May 2010); *Home Alone: Your Guide To Keeping Your Child Safe.*

Nzira,V. (2011); *Social Care With African Families In The UK.* Routledge.

Ramsey, R. (2002); *501 Ways to Boost Your Child's Self-esteem.* McGraw-Hill

Thompson, N. (2006); *Anti-discriminatory Practice* (2nd Ed.), Basingstoke: Macmillan.

White, R., Carr, P. and Lowe, N. (2002); The Children Act in Practice. UK Butterworths.

WEBSITES

http://www.cahealthadvocates.org/news/disparities/2005/discussion-race.html

www.cnpp.usda.gov/Publications/.../SymposiumBreakfastAndLearning.pdf breakfastpanel.org/children-and-learning/-

http://en.wikipedia.org/wiki/African_Charter_on_the_Rights_and_Welfare_of_the_Child

http://en.wikipedia.org/wiki/Trafficking_of_children

http://healthysleep.med.harvard.edu/healthy/matters/benefits-of-sleep

http://kidshealth.org/teen/your_mind/mental_health/depression.html#

http://longevity.about.com/od/lifelongenergy/tp/healthy_sleep.htm

http://racerelations.about.com/od/understandingrac1/a/internalizedracism.htm

http://stress.about.com/od/stresshealth/a/laughter.htm

http://stress.about.com/od/tensiontamers/a/stressrelievers.htm

http://www.100greatblackbritons.com/bios/stephen_lawrence.html

http://www.conqueringstress.com/how-to-handle-stress.html

http://www.fostering.org.uk/information/private_fostering.html

http://www.healthyforms.com/eating-right/benefits.php

http://www.helpguide.org/mental/depression_teen.htm

http://www.mumsnet.com/teenagers/depression

http://www.nhs.uk/Livewell/Goodfood/Pages/Healthyeating.aspx

http://www.nspcc.org.uk/Inform/resourcesforprofessionals/ctail/child_trafficking_advice_and_information_wda77600.html

http://www.privatefostering.org.uk/

http://www.rc.org/uer/InternalizedRacism.pdf

http://www.satsguide.co.uk/what_are_sats.htm

http://www.tranquilityisyours.com/

www.mayoclinic.com/health/depression/DS00175/DSECTION=symptoms

www.Parentsofdisabledchildren.co.uk

RESOURCE SECTION

Addaction

Offers a range of support developed for families and carers affected by substance misuse.

www.addaction.org.uk

Address: 67-69 Cowcross Street London EC1M 6PU

Tel. 020 7251 5860

Email: info@addaction.org.uk

Adfam

Works with families affected by drugs and alcohol, and supports carers of children whose parents have drug and alcohol problems.

www.adfam.org.uk

Address: 25 Corsham Street. London N1 6DR Tel: 020 7553 7640

Email: admin@adfam.org.uk

Advisory Centre for Education (ACE)

Offers free independent advice and information for parents and carers on a range of state education and schooling issues, including admissions, exclusion, attendance, special educational needs and bullying.

www.ace-ed.org.uk

Address: 1c Aberdeen Studios, 22 Highbury Grove, London N5 2DQ

General advice line: 0808 800 5793

Exclusion advice line: 0808 800 0327

Exclusion information line: 020 7704 9822 (24hr answer phone)

AFRUCA

This centre for African children and families in Greater Manchester is a specialist one-stop shop providing a range of prevention and early intervention projects and services.

Unit 98-100

23 New Mount Street

Manchester
M4 4DE
Tel: 0161 953 4711/4712

Black and Asian Therapists Online

Discusses mental health issues from a Black and Asian perspective and has a directory of Black and Asian counsellors and psychotherapists in the United Kingdom.
Website: www.baato.co.uk

BeGrand.net

Website offering information and advice to Grandparents, plus online and telephone advice.
www.begrand.net
Helpline: 0845 434 6835

Carers UK

Information and help for the UK's six million carers.
Tel: 020 7490 8818
Carers line: 0808 808 7777
Email: info@carersuk.org
Website: www.carersuk.org

Childhood Bereavement Network

Information, guidance and support for bereaved children and young people.
Tel: 020 7843 6309
Email: cbn@ncb.org.uk

ChildLine

Free national helpline for children and young people in danger and distress.
Helpline: 0800 1111
Textphone: 0800 400222
Website: www.childline.org.uk

Children's Legal Centre

Provides free independent legal advice and factsheets to children, parents, carers and professionals.

www.childrenslegalcentre.com   E-mail: clc@essex.ac.uk

Address: University of Essex, Wivenhoe Park, Colchester, Essex CO4 3SQ

Tel: 01206 877 910   Child Law Advice Line: 0808 802 0008

Community Legal Advice : 0845 345 4345

Citizens' Advice Bureaux

Helps people resolve their legal, monetary and other problems by providing free, independent and confidential advice through local bureaux and a website.

www.citizensadvice.org.uk

Contact a Family

Provides advice, information and support
to parents of all disabled children.
Tel: 0808 808 3555
Lines open Monday – Friday: 10am – 4pm
Monday evening 5.30pm – 7.30pm
www.cafamily.org.uk

thecoupleconnection

An interactive service where couples can find out how to manage their relationship more positively.
www.thecoupleconnection.net

Cruse Bereavement Care

Offers help to anyone who is bereaved. Free counselling, advice and publications.
Tel: 020 8939 9530
Day-by-day helpline: 0870 167 1677
Email: helpline@cruse.org.uk
Young persons' helpline: 0808 808 1677
Email: info@rd4u.org.uk
Website: www.crusebereavementcare.org.uk

Dad Talk

An online community where you can share ideas, find information and talk about the nitty-gritty issues of being a dad.

www.dadtalk.co.uk

Dads' Space & The 121 Space

No-nonsense info and advice for dads, and a safe and secure environment for parents to keep in touch with separated children.

www.dads-space.com

www.the121space.com

Debt Advisory Line

Debt Advice and expert confidential help

Tel: 0800 231 5860 and 0161 429 3313

Department for Education

Lists details of telephone help lines and online services to provide information, advice and support on a range of issues that parents and families may face in bringing up children and young people.

www.education.gov.uk/childrenandyoungpeople/families

Family Fund Trust

Helps families with severely disabled or seriously ill children to have choices and the opportunity to enjoy ordinary life. Gives grants for things that make life easier and more enjoyable for the disabled child and their family.

Address: 4 Alpha Court Monks Cross Drive York YO32 9WN

www.familyfund.org.uk

Tel: 0845 130 4542

Email: info@familyfund.org.uk

Family Mediation Helpline

Provides information and advice about family mediation services and eligibility for public funding.

www.familymediationhelpline.co.uk

Tel: 08456 026627

Family Rights Group (FRG)

Provides advice to parents and other family members whose children are involved with or require children's Social Care Services because of welfare needs or concerns. Publishes resources, helps to develop support groups for family, friends and carers, and runs a discussion board.

www.frg.org.uk

Address: Second Floor The Print House 18 Ashwin Street London E8 3DL

Tel: 020 7923 2628

Advice line: 0800 801 0366

Email: advice@frg.org.uk

Gingerbread

Provides support services, training and learning opportunities, and a campaigning voice for single parents.

Single Parent Helpline: 0800 018 5026

Lines open Monday – Friday: 9am – 5pm

Open until 8pm on Wednesdays

Gotateenager

A social networking site, run by Parentline Plus, giving help and advice to the parents of teenagers.

www.gotateenager.org.uk

The Grandparents' Association

Supports Grandparents and their families, especially those who have lost or are losing contact with their Grandchildren because of divorce, separation or other family problems; those caring for their Grandchildren on a full-time basis, and those with childcare responsibilities for their grandchildren.

www.grandparents-association.org.uk

Address: Moot House The Stow Harlow Essex CM20 3AG

Tel: 01279 428040

Helpline: 0845 434 9585

Welfare benefits advice and information: 0844 357 1033

Email: info@grandparents-association.org.uk

Grandparents Plus

Champions the role of Grandparents and the wider family in children's lives, especially when they take on the caring role in difficult family circumstances.

Address: Grandparents Plus 18 Victoria Park Square Bethnal Green London E2 9PF

Tel: 020 8981 8001

Email: info@grandparentsplus.org.uk

Home-Start

A network of nearly 16,000 trained parent volunteers who can help families with young children.

Freephone: 0800 068 63 68

Email: info@home-start.org.uk   Website: www.home-start.org.uk

International Organisation for Migration (IOM)

Runs a voluntary return scheme for those who want to return to their country including children and their families.

www.iomuk.org

11 Belgrave Road, London, SW1V 1RB

Tel: 0207 811 6000

Fax: 0207 811 6001

Mentor UK

Promotes the health and wellbeing of children and young people to reduce the damage that drugs can do to lives.

www.mentoruk.org.uk

Address: Fourth Floor 74 Great Eastern Street London EC2A 3JG

Tel: 020 7739 8494

Email: admin@mentoruk.org

Migrants Rights Charity

Working for the rights of all migrants in the United Kingdom.

www.migrantsrights.org.uk

Mind

Offers many services to those with mental health issues including help lines, drop-in centres, supported housing, counselling, befriending, advocacy, employment and training schemes.

Information line: 0845 766 0163

Email: contact@mind.org.uk

Website: www.mind.org.uk

The Money Advice Service

Free and Impartial advice on budgeting, borrowing, Savings and more

Tel: 0300 500 5000

National Black & Minority Ethnic Mental Health Network

To reduce inequality and promote good practice in mental health for racialised groups.

Tel: 020 7582 0400

Website: www.bmementalhealth.org.uk

National Family Mediation (NFM)

Provides mediation services to support couples who are separated, and their children and others affected by this.

www.nfm.org.uk

4, Barnfield Hill, Exeter EX1 1SR.

Tel: 0300 4000 636

Email: general@nfm.org.uk

Netmums

A locally based social networking site connecting parents with each other.

www.netmums.com

National Society for the Prevention of Cruelty to Children (NSPCC)

Helping to stop cruelty to children.

Helpline: 0808 800 5000

www.nspcc.org.uk

One Space

Interactive parenting resources, support and a lively online community for single parents from the Single Parent Action Network.

www.onespace.org.uk

Parentline Plus

A free and confidential helpline run by professionally-trained call takers – also parents – operating 24/7.

Tel: 0808 800 2222

Parents Against Drug Abuse (PADA)

Delivers support and services to the families of substance users, including a national helpline.

www.pada.org.uk

Address: The Foundry, Marcus Street Birkenhead CH41 1EU

Tel: 0151 649 1580

National Families Helpline: 08457 023867

Partners of Prisoners and Families Support Group

Operates helpline and provides a variety of services to support anyone who has a link with someone in prison, prisoners and other agencies.

www.partnersofprisoners.co.uk

Address: Valentine House 1079 Rochdale Road Blackley Manchester M9 8AJ

Tel: 0161 702 1000

Offenders' Families Helpline Tel: 0808 808 2003

Email: info@prisonersfamilieshelpline.co.uk

Prison Advice and Care Trust (PACT)

Provides practical and emotional support to prisoners and to their children and families. The Kinship Care Support Service provides support and advice to family members and friends who care for children whose parents are in HMP Holloway.

www.prisonadvice.org.uk

Address: Park Place 12 Lawn Lane Vauxhall London SW8 1UD

Telephone: 020 77359535

Refuge for Women and Children

Freephone 24-hour National Domestic Violence Helpline (run in partnership with Women's Aid and Refuge) Tel: 0808 2000 247 http://www.refuge.org.uk/

Refugee Council

Can provide information to refugees and their advisers

Telephone: 020 7346 6700

Website: http://www.refugeecouncil.org.uk

Relate

Aims to strengthen and maintain couple and family relationships by providing counselling and support.

www.relateforparents.org.uk

www.relate.org.uk

0300 100 1234

Respect

National Phone Line for Domestic Violence Perpetrators Helpline: 0845 122 8609

Retreat Association

Christian organisation promoting personal and religious retreats.

Tel: 020 7357 7736

Email: info@retreats.org.uk

Web: www.retreats.org.uk

Samaritans

Provides 24-hour, confidential emotional support to any person who is suicidal or despairing.

UK helpline: 0845 790 9090

ROI helpline: 1850 609 090

Website: www.samaritans.org.uk

SupportLine

Offers confidential emotional support for children, young adults and adults.

Helpline: 020 8554 9004

Email: info@supportline.org.uk

Website: www.supportline.org.uk

TalktoFrank

The government's national drugs helpline which offers free confidential drugs information and advice 24 hours a day. Information and advice are also available via the website.

www.talktofrank.com

24 hour advice line: 0800 77 66 00

Text: 82111 Email: frank@talktofrank.com

Voice

Advocacy organisation for children living away from home or in need.

www.voiceyp.org

Address: 320 City Road London EC1V 2NZ

Tel: 020 7833 5792

Young person's advice line: 0808 800 5792

Email: info@voiceyp.org

Women's Aid

Women's Aid is the key national charity working to end domestic violence against women and children. They support a network of over 500 domestic and sexual violence services across the UK.

Tel: 0808 200247

http://www.womensaid.org.uk/

Young Minds

Works to improve the emotional wellbeing and mental health of children and young people and empowering their parents and carers.

www.youngminds.org.uk

Address: 48-50 St John Street London EC1M 4DG

Tel: 020 7336 8445

Parents helpline: 0808 802 5544

YoungMinds Parents' Helpline

Free and confidential support for anyone worried about the emotional problems or behaviour of a child or young person up to the age of 25.

Tel: 0808 802 5544

Lines open Monday – Friday: 10am – 4pm

Wednesday evenings 6pm – 8pm

INDEX

For more information and to order
copies of this book visit:
www.africanparentsmustknow.com
www.authorhouse.co.uk
www.amazon.co.uk